AF576642

GRAND ALLUSIONS
ROBERT BARNES
LATE WORKS
1985–2015

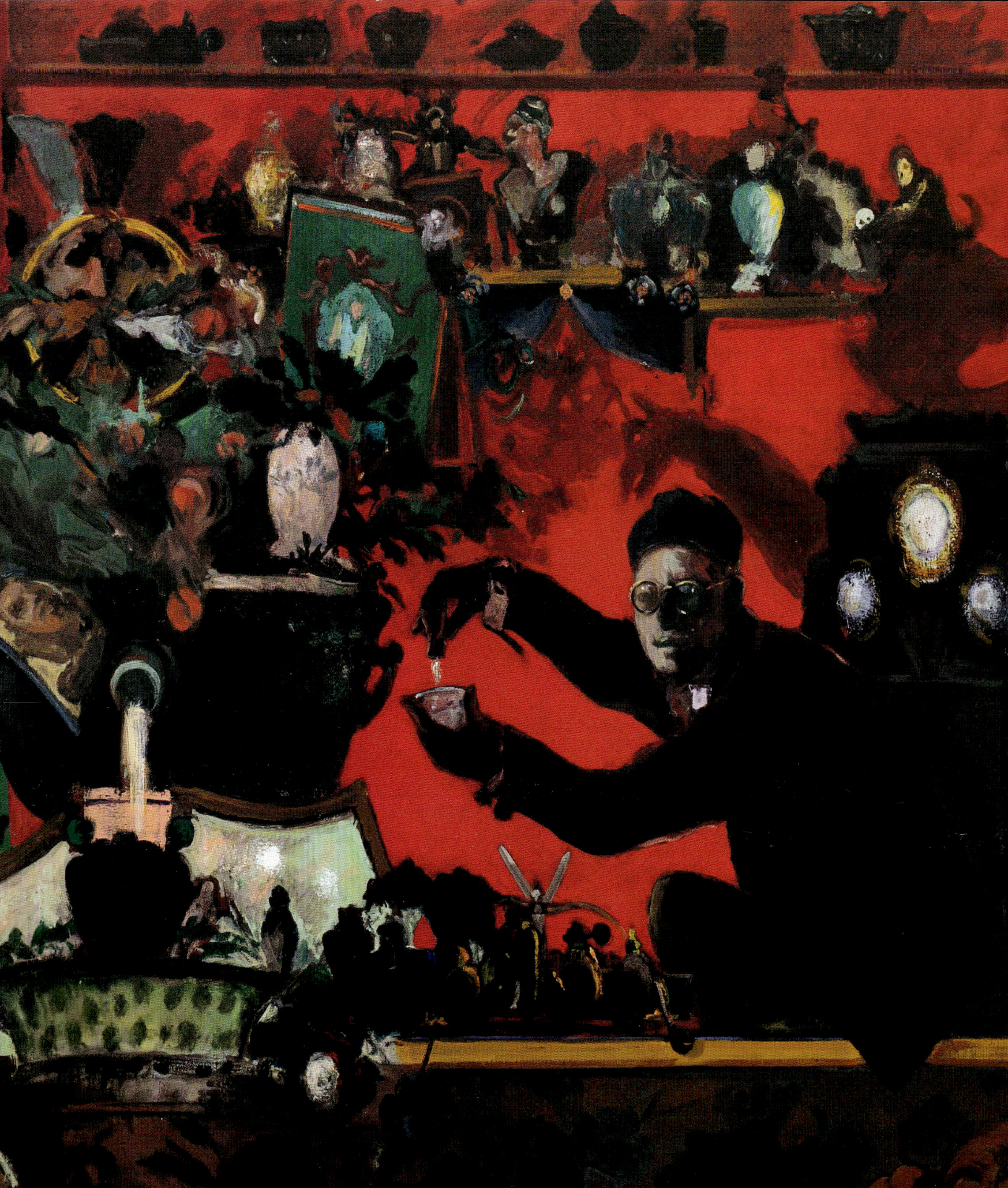

GRAND ALLUSIONS
ROBERT BARNES
LATE WORKS
1985–2015

MICHAEL ROOKS

INTRODUCTION BY DENNIS ADRIAN

CATALOGUE BY NANETTE ESSECK BREWER

INDIANA UNIVERSITY ART MUSEUM
IN ASSOCIATION WITH
INDIANA UNIVERSITY PRESS
BLOOMINGTON AND INDIANAPOLIS

This catalogue is published in conjunction with the special exhibition presented at the Indiana University Art Museum, Bloomington, September 26–December 20, 2015, curated by Nanette E. Brewer, the Lucienne M. Glaubinger Curator of Works on Paper, Indiana University Art Museum.

This publication was made possible with support from Patrick Duffy in honor of Wally Goodman, the Doris Steinmetz Kellett Endowed Fund for the Twentieth-Century Art Collection, the Henry and Gilda Buchbinder Family, the Morrow Family Foundation, Susan Thrasher, David H. Jacobs, Bill and Kay Carmichael, Joe and Sandy Morrow, Paul Caccia and Carmela Zammuto, Kenneth and Patricia Northcott, John Jones, Linda Alterwitz, Frank and Robin Schneider, the IU Art Museum's Arc Fund, and a Retired Faculty Grant-in-Aid, Office of the Vice Provost for Research, Indiana University.

Grand Allusions: Robert Barnes—Late Works 1985–2015
is distributed by
INDIANA UNIVERSITY PRESS
Office of Scholarly Publishing
Herman B Wells Library 350
1320 E. 13th Street, Bloomington, IN 47405-3907
iupress.indiana.edu
Tel: (800) 842-6796 (Toll-Free)
Tel: (812) 855-8817
Fax: (812) 855-8507

Library of Congress Cataloging-in-Publication Data

Rooks, Michael, author.
Grand allusions : Robert Barnes : late works, 1985-2015 / Michael Rooks ; Introduction by Dennis Adrian ; Catalogue by Nanette Esseck Brewer.
pages cm
"This catalogue is published in conjunction with the special exhibition presented at the Indiana University Art Museum, Bloomington, September 26-December 20, 2015 and curated by Nanette Esseck Brewer, the Lucienne M. Glaubinger Curator of Works on Paper, IU Art Museum."
Includes bibliographical references.
ISBN 978-0-253-01966-0
1. Barnes, Robert, 1934---Exhibitions. I. Brewer, Nanette Esseck. II. Adrian, Dennis, 1937- writer of introduction. III. Title.
N6537.B219A4 2015
759.13--dc23
2015028800

Produced by Indiana University Art Museum Publications, www.artmuseum.iu.edu

Designed by Brian Garvey
Edited by Linda Baden
Photography by Kevin Montague unless otherwise noted

Printed and bound in U.S.A.

Front cover
Mag Mell, 2010
Plate 33

Frontispiece
Molinard-Grasse (detail), 1996
Plate 8

Page 22
Arcadia (detail), 2010
Plate 34

Back cover
Self-Portrait Vanitas (detail), 2002
Plate 21

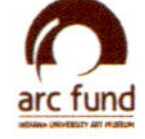

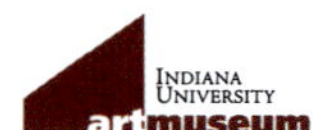

DEDICATED IN HONOR OF WALLY GOODMAN

EXHIBITION DONORS

Patrick Duffy in honor of Wally Goodman
The Doris Steinmetz Kellett Endowed Fund for the Twentieth-Century Art Collection
Henry and Gilda Buchbinder Family
Morrow Family Foundation
Susan Thrasher
David H. Jacobs
Bill and Kay Carmichael
Joe and Sandy Morrow
Paul Caccia and Carmela Zammuto
Kenneth and Patricia Northcott
John Jones
Linda Alterwitz
Frank and Robin Schneider

EXHIBITION LENDERS

Rolf Achilles and Maral Hashemi
Ani Afsar
Lawrence and Evelyn Aronson
Art Institute of Chicago
Robert Barnes and Corbett vs. Dempsey Gallery
Paul Caccia and Carmela Zammuto
Bill and Kay Carmichael
Jonas and Betsy Dovydenas
Laura and Larry Gerber
Estate of Ruth Horwich
Indiana University Art Museum
Indianapolis Museum of Art
John Jones
Willie Kohler and Shauna Angel Blue
Linda Kramer and Mary Kennedy
Kenneth and Patricia Northcott
Aileen and John Schloerb
David Sharpe and Anne Abrons
Smart Museum of Art, University of Chicago
Lolli Thurm
Lisa and Tim Wittman

CONTENTS

FOREWORDS

As one of my first responsibilities in my new role as director of the IU Art Museum, I am delighted to contribute to this celebration of Robert Barnes, an important American painter who for over thirty-five years shared his wisdom and talents with students and colleagues at Indiana University as a distinguished professor of painting in the Henry Radford Hope School of Fine Arts. The exhibition *Grand Allusions: Robert Barnes—Late Works 1985–2015* surveys the most recent decades of the artist's work through thirty-eight oil paintings, pastels, and caseins, and it is the first major exhibition of this distinguished former colleague to be undertaken by our museum. I share director emerita Heidi Gealt's joy in presenting this long overdue exhibition of Robert Barnes's works in our galleries.

I am a newcomer to Bloomington and a specialist in older European art, so the work of Robert Barnes is a revelation to me. Perhaps because of my background, I find his art engaging and profound. The term allusion means an expression that calls something to mind without explicitly referring to it. As Michael Rooks observes in his essay for this catalogue, Barnes achieves his grand allusions by infusing dynamic painterly compositions with erudite mythic, literary, art-historical, and autobiographical references. The resulting paintings are highly complex but indirect visual narratives that are beautiful and sensuous and mysterious and ultimately full of meaning.

Barnes works are not easily understood without careful observance of his techniques and diligent study of his rarified subject matter. Facilitating an experience that enables and fosters close looking and deep thinking is the job of the university museum, and I thank the artist for entrusting the Indiana University Art Museum to present this significant portion of his life's work to the world. I would also like to take this opportunity to thank the lenders to the exhibition for sharing their treasures with us. Finally, I would like to acknowledge Nanette Esseck Brewer, the museum's Lucienne M. Glaubinger Curator of Works on Paper, for her strong and inspired leadership as curator of this excellent exhibition and its accompanying catalogue.

David A. Brenneman
The Wilma E. Kelley Director,
Indiana University Art Museum

When Robert Barnes retired in 1999 after thirty-five years of teaching, he deferred a retrospective exhibition at the IU Art Museum of the kind that had celebrated the careers of many of his colleagues, including Alma Eikerman, Karl Martz, Rudy Pozzatti, and Barry Gealt. By then, Bob had developed a reputation among curators and museums that had led to a mid-career retrospective organized by the Madison (Wisconsin) Art Center that opened in New York City in 1985 and traveled to Indianapolis, Madison, Chicago, and Miami—but sadly, not to Bloomington. The current exhibition corrects this omission, focusing on the works Bob has produced since 1985. This catalogue, which accompanies the exhibition, gives me the opportunity to speak both as a museum director and as an art historian in expressing my appreciation for Bob's work as a narrative artist.

I share the opinion of the critics and collectors who regard Robert Barnes as one of the best visual storytellers of his generation. Bob's gifts as an imaginative and engaging pictorial narrator link him to a long line of artists who have given visual shape to narratives tracing back to the beginning of art-making. From the primeval visions of hunters and their prey with which European cave dwellers adorned the subterranean walls of Lascaux, to the scene of the dead hero Sarpedon so movingly depicted on the Euphronios Krater of ca. 515 BC, painters, sculptors and draftsmen have taken the events that shaped their world and given them visual form. Each of them added their perspective on the human condition. We are mortal, we are alternately frail or mighty, cowardly or brave, selfish and selfless, loving or hateful, despairing or hopeful. We are flawed and we seek perfection.

Since the first epic narratives, the Iliad and the Odyssey, were told around 1260 BC, the supply of stories available to visual artists has grown enormously. After ancient myths and Biblical texts came tales from the likes of Ovid, Dante, Boccaccio, and Shakespeare, followed by innumerable writers from Goethe to Dickens, whose stories entranced successive generations of readers. In the sixteenth century, artists sometimes felt free to add their own stories and experiences to the vast repertoire of commonly known tales. By the seventeenth century, the incidents of ordinary life became popular means to express both the positive and negative impulses that govern human behavior.

Until the arrival of film, the format for most artists was a single image through which an event was related, although those who painted murals, or decorated predellas, or used multiple sheets of paper had the latitude to let a story unfold over more than one scene. As artists' training shifted from studies with a master or in a workshop to the academy, the highest level an artist could reach was the visual depiction of a grand heroic tale generally based on mythology or a momentous historic occasion, featuring a male or female nude. For post-academic artists, including the Impressionists, more humble and quotidian incidents were preferred; but whether on a grand scale or a modest one, the impulse among artists to tell stories continued, while audiences studied their visual chronicles with as much enthusiasm as they enjoyed the serial narratives issued regularly by the likes of Dickens and Trollope.

By the twentieth century, many of the structures that had unified culture and art began to come apart, in some ways separating artist from their viewers, and in other ways liberating artists and offering them a vast new array of choices. Some moved in the direction of pure abstraction; others, like Picasso, chose to develop their own pictographic language to relate the many events, some mythic, some personal, which they wanted to portray. The literary canon that had once assured artists that the characters and incidents they placed on canvas or carved in marble would be universally understood was no longer the unifying resource it had been in the past. Artists who chose to tell stories selected from a nearly inexhaustible realm of source material, sometimes from literature, but just as likely from their own experiences, including their dreams or nightmares, their loves and hatreds. Some, like N. C. Wyeth, specialized in illustrating well-known books; others, like Salvador Dalí, mined their subconscious. By the second half of the twentieth century and into the twenty-first, however, the notion of storytelling itself was often rejected by artists as no longer relevant.

Robert Barnes, whose visual storytelling began in the 1960s, belongs to a generation of artists who strongly believed in narrative, but who could not and did not expect their audiences to know exactly what story was being told in any given work. Barnes has established a special niche for himself by virtue of his gift for exquisite color and lyrical form; yet it is his nearly insatiable appetite for describing incidents, many obscure or arcane, that sets him apart from his peers. He is a miner of abstruse literary veins, including the Celtic myths of his ancestors and the biographies of people who interest him, selectively choosing to depict themes that run through literature and life.

No matter what his subject, Barnes presents the viewer with a visual banquet. He is a master of the exuberant, the lavish, the opulent, the vibrant, and the exotic. Seeing his work is to experience the longing to possess, since his images are irresistibly gorgeous. His work entices the viewer to learn more about his stories to better appreciate his choices of characters, landscape, flora, and fauna. Paradoxically, his narration arises from his formal constructs: he finds stories to give meaning and direction to his germinal impulse to balance color, shape, form, and texture. Viewers depend on the titles of his paintings to access his meaning, although in some cases no title is necessary: *Eden* (2010; plate 32), for instance, tells the Genesis story in a progression of vignettes, relying on lush, exotic foliage and age-old symbols to carry the narrative . All the meaning of the story is in the picture, and in this case, the title may be superfluous.

His *Mag Mell* (2010; plate 33) is a ravishing image of nature's bounty, an Irish heaven in which the fish practically leap into the fishermen's boats as they rise from the water against a molten sky. In this work, the title does add meaning and links us to the world of Celtic fable and myth. As readers of this catalogue and visitors to the exhibition will see, Robert Barnes has an almost limitless capacity for narrative, his range spanning the personal and quotidian to the epic and heroic.

Adelheid M. Gealt
Director Emerita, Indiana University Art Museum

ACKNOWLEDGEMENTS

When he wasn't teaching, Robert Barnes preferred to devote himself to the act of creating, rather than maintaining an archive. He was blessed to have found excellent artist representation from the very beginning of his professional career. Unfortunately, some of those dealers eventually went out of business or passed away suddenly, and, therefore, many of their records are no longer available. As such, much of the research for this exhibit involved the re-discovery of the locations of Barnes's works, even those that were produced during the past three decades. My thanks go to Bob Hiebert and Sidney Block, the proprietors of Printworks, Inc., who gave me my first clues to many of the Chicago-based Barnes collectors.

These passionate collectors, many of whom have lent work to the exhibition (see page vi for a full list of lenders), not only shared their stories and love of Barnes's work, but also provided names and contact information for other collectors. Barnes's other current dealers, John Corbett and Jim Dempsey and their staff, likewise, offered valuable assistance and encouragement, as did Yolanda Farias at Carl Hammer Gallery. Museum professionals, including Debora Wood at the Mary and Leigh Block Museum of Art; Richard Born and Alice Kain at the Smart Museum of Art; Jude Palmese at the Museum of Contemporary Art, Chicago; Sarah Urist Green at the Indianapolis Museum of Art; Craig Hadley at the Richard E. Peeler Art Center at DePauw University; Rachel Perry and Mark Ruschman at the Indiana State Museum; and Nora Riccio, Natasha Derrickson, and Suzanne Folds McCullagh at the Art Institute of Chicago, graciously shared their Barnes holdings and their curatorial records.

Among the many collectors who provided information about their collection (and, often, their hospitality) are Patrick Duffy, Henry and Gilda Buchbinder, Bill and Kay Carmichael, Paul Caccia and Carmela Zammuto, Kenneth and Patricia Northcott, Rolf Achilles and Maral Hashemi, Lawrence and Evelyn Aronson, Jonas and Betsy Dovydenas, Richard Born and Dennis Adrian, Laura and Larry Gerber, the late Ruth Horwich, John Jones, Willie Kohler and Shauna Angel Blue, Linda Kramer and Mary Kennedy, Aileen and John Schloerb, David Sharpe and Anne Abrons, Lolli Thurm, Ani Afsar, Lisa and Tim Wittman, Sharon and Richard Carlson, John and Anne Heinz, Jane Potter Otten, Lisa Audi, Whitney Allen, Merrie Faye Witkin, Dr. Sheldon Kirshner and Jan Baiden, Pam Morris, Dennis Rosenthal, Rosa Ana Orlando of the Roy and Mary Cullen Art Collection, and Elizabeth K. Whiting at the Union League Club of Chicago.

The museum's director emerita Heidi Gealt and the museum's development staff, particularly Patty Winterton, have worked tirelessly to keep this project alive. Their passion attracted many private donors, who are listed in full on page vi. We could not have done this project without them.

Like all exhibitions, there are many museum staff members involved. I would like to thank several others who have been especially involved with this publication: Kevin Montague, Brian Garvey, Linda Baden, Anita Bracalente, Heather Hales, Diane Pelrine, and graduate assistants Shi Li and Assefa Dibaba. At IU Press, my thanks go to Linda Oblack and Sarah Jacobi.

I am also grateful to our guest authors Michael Rooks, the Wieland Family Curator of Modern and Contemporary Art at the High Museum of Art, and Dennis Adrian, independent scholar, who have written about and been the standard bearers for Barnes's work over many years.

Lastly, I must gratefully acknowledge Robert Barnes and his wife Nancy, who have put up with my many phone calls and generously shared their time and stories with me over many years. It has been a wonderful artistic scavenger hunt with a most rewarding prize.

Nanette Esseck Brewer
The Lucienne M. Glaubinger Curator of Works on Paper
Indiana University Art Museum

COLLECTORS' APPRECIATION

The collectors of Robert Barnes's paintings recognize his contributions as an artist and as a visual storyteller, but they do not place him in a particular "box" despite his many years exhibiting mainly in Chicago, a city that supports a strong group of marvelous artists many of whom are important narrators as well. Both in terms of style as well as content, Bob's approach to form and color links him back to a long and venerable pictorial tradition—it is no accident that Bob and Nancy own a house in Italy (Umbertide), and that Titian, among other masters, is revered by him. Some collectors recognize his connection to that great artistic past. Yet Bob's work transcends geography and in many ways, transcends time, linking him to a timeless tradition of great painting. Many collectors have affirmed as much. What follows are brief notes of high praise and thoughtful assessment from several of those collectors.

Adelheid M. Gealt
Director Emerita, Indiana University Art Museum

As a collector, often you fall head over heels with an artist's work. The sheer delight and of course the eventual desire has fueled collecting in the art world I guess for centuries. Is it curiosity, compulsion or maybe just being a collector that you really know this work speaks to the collection and is a perfect fit, much like a puzzle?

Wally Goodman taught me about collecting, Wally Goodman taught me how to live an extraordinary life with art and especially, but not often, also knowing the artist. He had a gift with artists that almost doesn't exist in the current art world; or certainly limits the abilities of many collectors to converse with the creator/maker/instigator of the work. The artist! He loved artists, and artists were drawn to him, I learned the value of this priceless and often sensitive connection.

We met Robert at Sonia Zaks Gallery at an opening in maybe 1998/1999? It was the magic of friendship and the love of the artist at the first moments of conversation. When we left, Wally and I were gob smacked with him and especially his work....Our curiosity, compulsion and belief in this artist continues today, and assuredly tomorrow. We then donated a work to the IU Art Museum in Robert's honor, and the friendship deepened.

I know Wally, who passed in January 2008, would endorse my every word to describe the journey of Wally Goodman, Patrick Duffy, and Robert Barnes. Especially, Robert's immense heart and talent. —*Patrick Duffy*

Robert Barnes is a fearless painter who has created a theatre of decisive moments that revel in shadow and oblique action. He is a storyteller, highly intellectual, and sexy. Without regard for trends, Robert Barnes stands alone, a triumphant, enigmatic Magus presenting us with works that defy reality and exist as vividly hot incantations.
—Rolf Achilles

We bought and enjoy Bob's art because it is bold, bright, vibrant, colorful, and tells an interesting story—just like him. Viewing one of his works is like being with him.
—Bill and Kay Carmichael

A great artist develops a vocabulary with the marks he creates. That vocabulary tells a story which asks questions about the condition of life. The viewer of his work answers those questions with questions of his own. This continual dialogue, in our opinion, is what makes a work of art significant.

We see this dialogue in Vincent Van Gogh's works. We see his inner thoughts and constantly learn who the man is.

After living with some of Bob Barnes work for over thirty-seven years, we are convinced that he carries on that tradition. Bob's art is dynamic and alive and continues to push the viewers' inner thoughts.

That, to us, is a sign of greatness! *—Evie and Larry Aronson*

Bob is a fascinating person and artist. It was amazing to see the works be created when the crunch time came before an exhibition. I loved the feelings of the people in his painting. You can feel the emotion, the personality, and the life they lived in his works.
—Steve Ferguson

Living with Bob's paintings and watercolors over many years continues to deepen our appreciation of both him and his work—no doubt about it, Bob is a great artist.
—Gilda and Henry Buchbinder

Like many great artists, Barnes is capable of making wonderful works on a very small scale as well as on large canvasses. This was a godsend when I started collecting 42 years ago and had limited means. Amen. *—Lolli Thurm*

INTRODUCTION: ROBERT BARNES AND VISIONARY ACTUALITY

DENNIS ADRIAN

For more than fifty years, the American painter Robert Barnes has presented a seemingly unending series of visionary works, which arise from a profound imagination and sense of fantasy. Despite the dizzying richness of the artist's inventive and unexpected imagery, Barnes's major works (oil, gouache, casein, and pastels) nevertheless usually are grounded in historical, literary, and artistic subjects. These are of a peculiar kind, including alchemy; secret clubs and societies; artistic associations and movements such as Dada; English Romantic poets and writers; and artists specializing in the bizarre, the fantastic, the mythical, and the hermetically arcane worlds of religious history, myths, and legends.

The artist's fascination with the strange and obscure is manifested in a complex pictorial style that itself is theatrical and densely nuanced. All of Barnes's work is permeated with complex allusions to different painterly traditions: those associated with Titian, Rubens, Velasquez, Goya, and Manet; various directions in Mannerist art; James Ensor and related nineteenth-century traditions; and such modern investigations and byways as Surrealism, Scuola Metafisica, and mysterious allegories of little-known themes and subjects. All of these idiosyncrasies and a personal taste for the outré are inextricably invested with a bravura handling of paint, an extraordinary sense of color, and a genius for intricate formal inventions.

It is useful to point out that Barnes has many connections with Marcel Duchamp, Matta, the influential dealer Julien Levy, H. C. Westermann, and June Leaf, to name just a few of Barnes's wide circles of artistic and literary associations. These affinities also include personages from history or literature possessing notable individual quirks of taste and poetic images of powerful eccentricity, many with colorful and strange biographies. Notable among these are such figures as Beau Brummell, Percy Shelley and his immediate English Romantic circle, the early American botanist John Bartram, Tristan Tzara, Ezra Pound, the photographer and dealer Alfred Stieglitz, the Byronic adventurer Edward Trelawney, master parfumeurs of France, Joseph Wright of Derby, Old Jolyon (Jon Galsworthy's patriarch of *The Forsyte Saga*), the German "Wild Boy" of the 1820s named Kaspar Hauser, and a host of other eccentrics, loners, outsiders, mystics, prophets, and peculiar souls.

Barnes's recent works have to do with the history and principal personalities of Chicago's literary, artistic, and political association named the Dil [sic] Pickle Club, which flourished in various locales on the near north side of the city from around 1914 to 1935. (A comprehensive history of the Dil Pickle Club is yet to be written, though there are some published fragmentary memoirs by habitués. The club published a magazine and issued broadsheets about its activities and programs.) There were novelists, writers, artists, and soapbox orators, hoboes, and other oddballs. Some memorable personalities associated with the club at various times were Sherwood Anderson, Djuna Barnes, Clarence Darrow, Katherine Dunham, Jun Fujita, Ben Hecht, Kenneth Rexroth, Carl Sandburg, and the designer Edgar Miller. To these and others the Dil Pickle Club offered indifferent food, musical performances, theatrical ventures in a tiny theater space, art exhibitions, uninhibited discussions on leftist political issues, free love, and liberal causes such as the cases of Sacco and Vanzetti, the Scottsboro Boys, and many others. This radical political complexion was determined by the club's founder, the former Wobbly John "Jack" Jones, and others.

The Dil Pickle Club motto (painted just outside the entrance door)—Step High, Stoop Low and Leave Your Dignity Outside—gives a tangy whiff of the spirit and attitudes of the place. This rapscallion flavor is an ideal stimulus for Barnes's unfettered gifts of fantasy, imagination, and inventiveness. Barnes' utilization of tableau-like settings is related to his interest in and regard for theatrical devices such as divided planes that show several aspects of the scene, permitting multiple symbolic views of the settings, subjects, and "cast of characters." The presentation of the themes in tipped and overlapping sections provides a sense of action occurring through segments of time, analogous to cinematic effects such as montages and collage.

This way of breaking up and into the action and settings of Barnes's tableaux gives the viewer a sensation of movement and life, both visionary and descriptive. When Barnes's remarkable use of colors that glow like embers is added to his dense working of his materials, one enters a vividly poetic world in which ordinary experience is heightened to rare states of awareness and perception. In this way Barnes catches what might be called a flowing sense of transient permanence composed of memory, active perception, and imagination. For Barnes, then, the numinous and complex nature of artistic perception presents magical visions that are inexhaustible sources of revelation and delight.

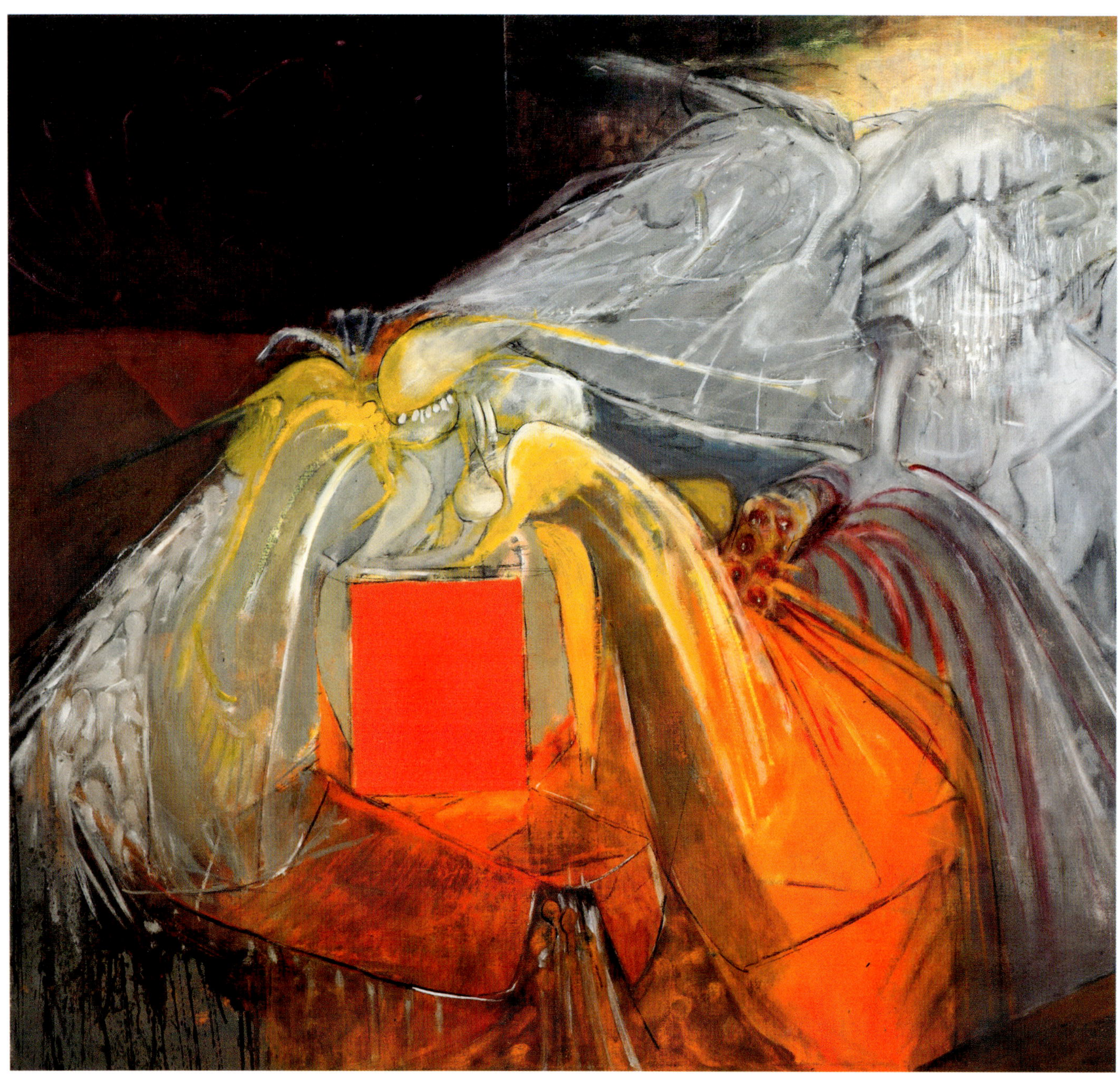

Fig. 1 Robert Barnes (American, b. 1934) and Roberto Matta (Chilean, 1911–2002). **Lucifer, Son of Mourning**, 1956. Oil on canvas. Private collection, Chicago

GRAND ALLUSIONS

ROBERT BARNES

LATE WORKS

1985–2015

MICHAEL ROOKS

G*rand Allusions—Robert Barnes* surveys the artist's work of the last three decades, presenting a selection of paintings, including works in casein and pastel, whose subjects are based upon literary, mythological, folkloric, and artistic personages or ideas. The work comprises a Fellini-esque dreamscape populated by a cast of characters who are invented and real, allegorical and historical, otherworldly and human—including Barnes himself. Barnes's work provides a platform for the exploration of his literary erudition, art historical biases and musings, fantasies, and idiosyncratic oddball interests. He summons improbable, incredible images with well-crafted visual turns of phrase, like a great Scots storyteller over a glass of whiskey. At the same time, the bold materiality of Barnes's paintings imbues them with a visceral power that is direct and unflinching.

Barnes has practiced the discipline of painting for more than fifty years. He describes painting in existential terms, and he communicates the exigency of this discipline by way of his painting's seductive surfaces, which are the result of his experimentation and tenacity in the studio as he works to master new materials and techniques. With rapid, urgent brushwork and an instinctive understanding of the palpable, fleshy properties of paint, Barnes brings into accord the intellectual and artistic images that occupy his imagination and a painterly sensibility that recalls the European Grand Manner of centuries past.

More often than not, his protagonists are stand-ins for Barnes himself who reveal something of the artist's own life story and ethos, from the fiercely provocative proto-Dada poet and boxer Arthur Cravan, to the early American anthropologist William Bartram, to the eccentric actor and painter Paul Swan, to the Irish mythic hero Finn McCall, to ancient daemons—all of whom represent outsiders or outliers and who are usually mischievous, creative spirits. They share with Barnes an inescapable need to explore, invent, or create, often through disruption, rebellion, and opposition, embodying the idea of individualism to an extent that they become iconoclastic, symbolic figures.

Grand Allusions picks up where Barnes's 1985 retrospective exhibition left off. That show, organized by the Madison Art Center, encompassed his career from his early work (1956–1964), when Barnes was under the sway of mentors such as Marcel Duchamp and Chilean-born surrealist Matta (Roberto Matta Echaurren), to the work of his early maturity (1965–1984) after he had begun teaching at Indiana University's Henry Radford Hope School of Fine Arts. In these first three decades of Barnes's career, the formal structure of his work was characterized by the spatial fracturing of the picture plane; by the modulation of form through an underlying system of automatic drawing that describes unnamable but oddly familiar things; and by the active interplay of light, shadow, and color. The work of the most recent three decades presented in *Grand Allusions* is characterized by a dynamic sense of expansion and compression of space through dramatic contrasts of light and dark; by highly keyed color; and by the occurrence of non-linear passages, shifting rhythmically between open and closed forms, produced with gestural marks that at times approach abstraction.

Grand Allusions includes works produced in pastel and casein in addition to large works in oil-based media from the past several decades, representing these important and reciprocal modes of painting for Barnes. He first used pastels for a series based on Ezra Pound's *Cantos* in 1961. Acquiring an understanding of the techniques of *pastellistes* such as Jean Baptiste Chardin and Edgar Degas through experimentation and research, Barnes has gained a mastery of this delicate, laborious, and potentially noxious medium that is uncommon among contemporary painters. Like the *pastellistes*, he uses pastels like paint, layering pigments, securing them with fixative, scraping and sanding them away, and then applying more layers over them until images began to suggest themselves, while achieving a rich tapestry of color, value, and intensity.

Likewise, Barnes has employed casein and watercolor in his practice since the 1960s, gaining a command of their fluid properties for compositions in which space becomes elastic and liquid like the materials themselves, and color becomes more saturated and unmodulated or flatter than in his larger paintings, which tend to possess a broader range of value and a higher degree of intensity than the caseins. Barnes's pastels, caseins, and watercolors of the past several decades have served in some respects to provide stages in his exploration of subjective or formal ideas that are fleshed out in the larger paintings. But more recently, Barnes's approach to the use of materials and processes has coalesced. For example, in paintings such as *Wobblies* (2011; plate 35), *Poetry Reading at the Dil* (2012; plate 36), and *Honeymoon on Lake Michigan* (2012; plate 37), Barnes combines pastel and casein in order to achieve a surface that is both dry and liquid with a physical range from chalky to viscous.

Barnes usually works on five or six large paintings concurrently, each individual work spurring formal and thematic motifs in the next. The large paintings often are followed by a group of smaller works on paper. Practical reasons limit him to working in only one medium at a time in these campaigns, since the unique physical properties of each medium require a different set-up; this also allows Barnes to immerse himself in the physical, sensory language of each medium. By working on many paintings at once, Barnes develops a formal continuity among the paintings in a group or series. In the series *Blood and Perfume*, for example, the sharp contrast of light and dark establishes a shadowy undercurrent in each painting, conveying the ethereal nature of their subject—olfaction—while exploiting the rich, deep tonalities of oil-based pigments. In the more recent group of casein paintings related to theatrical spaces, including *Chinese Opera* and *The Yiddish Theater* (both 2009; plates 28 and 29), one may trace the recurring formal device of undulating lines running horizontally from one scene to the next, establishing divisions that suggest the spaces of the stage, the orchestra pit, and the audience, while also creating a pulsating rhythm that connects each work in the series.

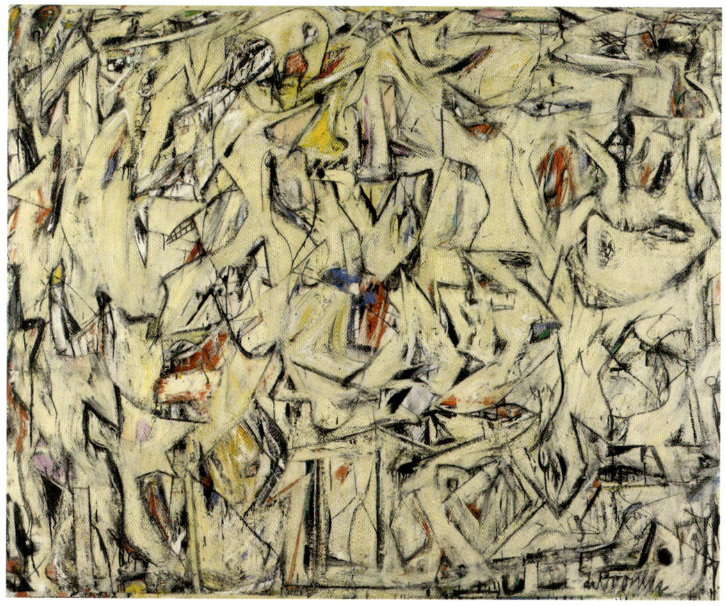

Fig. 2 Willem de Kooning (American, 1904–1997). **Excavation**, 1950. Oil on canvas. The Art Institute of Chicago, Mr. and Mrs. Frank G. Logan Purchase Prize Fund; restricted gifts of Edgar J. Kaufmann, Jr., and Mr. and Mrs. Noah Goldowsky, 1952.1 ©2015 The Willem de Kooning Foundation/Artists Rights Society (ARS), New York

The Language of Abstraction

Since the time he emerged from the School of the Art Institute of Chicago in the 1950s, Robert Barnes has been considered one of his generation's most idiosyncratic artists, eluding placement within the larger context of representational or narrative painting. He is more oriented than almost any of his peers towards utilizing literary and theatrical devices, including multiple and shifting perspectives, foreshadowing, soliloquy and narration, internal and external dialogue, and the conjuring of dramatic imagery. Yet, perhaps because abstraction is, ultimately, the grammar of Barnes's painting, he never aligned himself with any of the various modes of realism that attended the return of figurative painting in post-war American art.

Barnes would begin a painting with objectiveless, agitated charcoal markings on prepared canvas, which served as a manner of mapping out the formal elements of movement and space and establishing an abstract framework for color and light. He would then reinforce this all-over structure by laying on thin washes, then applying thicker layers of paint, which he scraped away until a critical tension between formal and figurative impulses was achieved—what he would later describe as a metaphorical "marshalling of forces." In the process, themes and subjects would become clearer and more specific. This underlying abstract structure remains an important organizational system that governs Barnes's compositions and manifests itself with even greater presence in work since the mid-1980s, wherein images emerge from and recede into an open, all-over network of marks and planes of color, resulting in a complex spatial logic.

Yet, while abstraction has been the foundation of Barnes's painterly language from the outset, the preliminary modes of abstraction in Barnes's studio practice have always engendered fantastic narrative images. This was the result of his cultivation of biomorphic imagery through spontaneous drawing advocated by Matta and recalling the fantastic images of Joan Miró and Arshile Gorky (who was himself encouraged by Matta to draw instinctively). It distinguished Barnes from both abstract artists as well as from representational painters when he emerged in the late 1950s.

With notable exceptions—such as the psychologically taut work of Francis Bacon (with whom Barnes briefly studied), the realism of Fairfield Porter and the later New Perceptual Realists of the 1950s, and the painterly figuration of David Hockney and Alex Katz—representational painting occupied a place of alterity in the space of contemporary art discourse until the emergence of neo-expressionism in the 1980s. Since the predominance of Greenbergian formalism, representational painting—objective, figurative, and narrative—has never received the same degree of respect as have prevailing contemporaneous aesthetics such as the countless reduplicative forms of abstraction since midcentury, or conceptual practices and process-based art making. Today, abstraction, not figuration, remains the most popular form of painting almost three-quarters of a century after Abstract Expressionism.

All this is to say that Robert Barnes is not a fashionable painter and never has been. Barnes has always sought to position himself outside the mainstreams of contemporary art. Throughout his career he has been defiant, working, as he might prefer to say, in opposition to the status quo. In this, at the outset of his career, he was not alone. At the School of the Art Institute of Chicago he met classmate H. C. Westermann who, along with Leon Golub, embodied the rebellious defiance of "the Chicago School"—the city's emergent postwar art scene—and challenged the preeminence of New York abstraction and the authority of the art world establishment by making psychologically layered and nuanced figurative work.

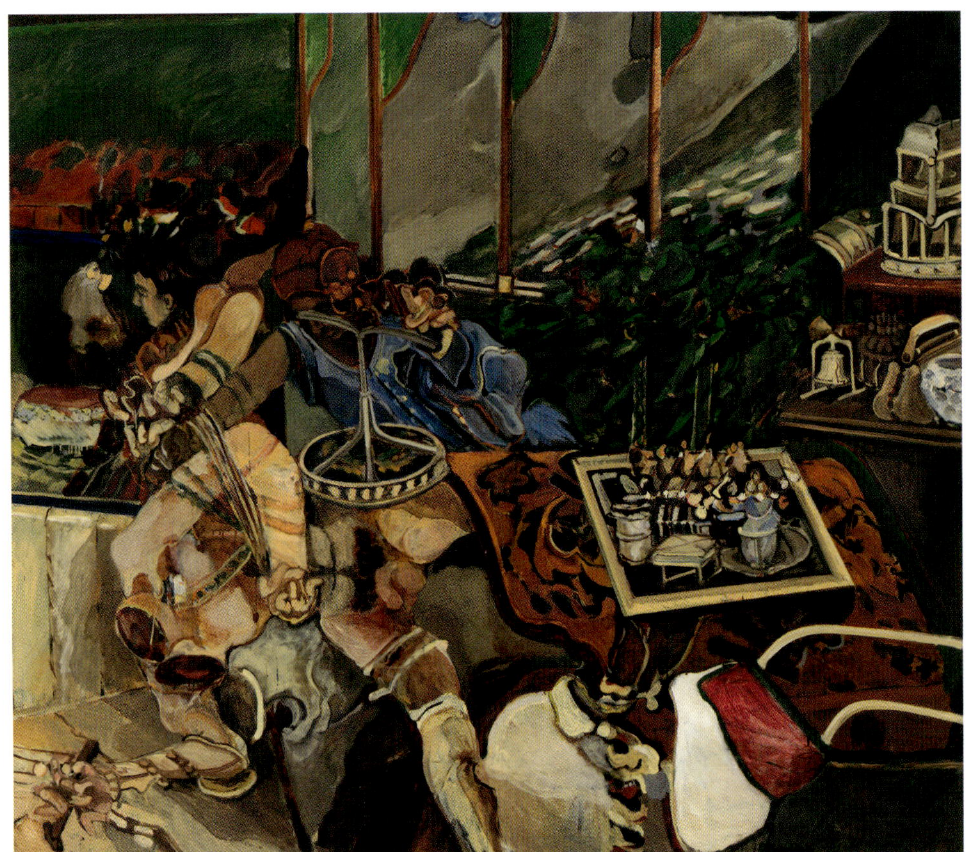

Fig. 3 Robert Barnes (American, b. 1934). **Judith and Holofernes,** 1958. Oil on canvas. Whitney Museum of Art, New York; Purchase, with funds from the Sumner Foundation Purchase Award, 61.48. Digital image ©Whitney Museum of American Art, N.Y.

Biography

Barnes arrived in Chicago as a teenager, but with the diverse life experiences of an adult. He was born in Washington DC in 1934, where he was raised by his paternal grandfather, Merton Barnes. His uncommon middle name, Myrddyn, derived from the legendary Welsh visionary Myrddin Wyllt (a prototype for the wizard Merlin), portended Barnes's later interest in the arcane, literary, esoteric, mysterious, and mythological. Upon the death of his grandfather in 1950, Barnes was enrolled by his parents at the Virginia Military Institute, but he ran away after six months and hitchhiked to Texas and Arizona, where he worked odd jobs in exchange for food and lodging. In Arizona he was welcomed onto a reservation of the Navajo Nation.

Barnes left Arizona for the Chicago suburb of Wilmette where, for a short time, he managed to live within the confines of a strained relationship with his parents, graduating from New Trier High School in 1952. Around this time he became interested in painting and soon struck out on his own to the south side of Chicago, where he pursued an independent life learning to paint, reading poetry, and boxing. He found a bartending job in a nightclub called the Kiosk, where he met author and poet Jessica Nelson North.[1] Taken with Barnes, she enrolled him in a poetry class at the University of Chicago taught by the poet Paul Carroll. In Carroll's class, Barnes was introduced to Irish authors and poets and gravitated toward the work of James Joyce, John Millington Synge, and William Butler Yeats.

Inspired by the works of drama he studied, Barnes considered acting classes at the Goodman School of Drama, which was then affiliated with the School of the Art Institute of Chicago (SAIC).[2] Instead, he enrolled in art classes at SAIC and was accepted for admission in the fall of 1952. He did, however, continue to nurture a passionate interest in the theater, which became an enduring and recurring subject in his work.

At SAIC Barnes studied with influential art historians Kathleen Blackshear and Whitney Halsted, and with painters Paul Wieghardt and Isobel Steele MacKinnon, who had been a student of Hans Hofmann. Blackshear introduced Barnes to the anthropology and archaeology collections at the Field Museum of Natural History and the Oriental Institute at the University of Chicago, while Halsted taught the history of what was then called "primitive art." Wieghardt's subdued earth-tone palette, sophisticated draftsmanship, and classical compositions resonate in the sobriety of Barnes's early work, while Hans Hofmann's concept of spatial dynamism through the use of overlapping planes, explicated by MacKinnon, had a tremendous impact on Barnes, fostering a sense of elastic, spatial complexity that has always been a hallmark of his work.

In 1955 Roberto Matta became a close friend and mentor to Barnes, and through his influence Barnes began working in a manner unique to his own way of seeing and thinking [fig. 1]. Initially, Barnes's work was abstract, influenced by the tonal contrast of Franz Kline and the gestural brushwork of Willem de Kooning, but then it became more figurative. Soon Barnes had developed a technique and style that he described as a manner of "excavating" figurative images by way of abstraction from within the rectangle of the painting, in reference to de Kooning's painting *Excavation* [fig. 2].[3]

After receiving his bachelor of fine arts degree in 1956, Barnes moved to New York, where he apprenticed with Matta and studied art history at Hunter College. Matta introduced Barnes to influential figures including Marcel Duchamp, William Copley, Tristan Tzara, Max Ernst, Salvador Dali, and Julien Levy, and Barnes was a frequent guest at Duchamp's New York apartment, where the two would play chess.[4] Duchamp encouraged Barnes's penchant for making literary connections in his art, introducing him to the works of French writers such as Blaise Cendrars, Jean Cocteau, Joris-Karl Huysmans, Stéphane Mallarmé, and Arthur Rimbaud.

Around that time, Barnes began showing his paintings regularly in New York and Chicago, and he was hired by Indiana University in 1961 to teach graduate-level painting for two summer sessions. That year he was also included in the Whitney Museum's Annual Exhibition, winning a Sumner Foundation Purchase Award for his large painting *Judith and Holofernes*, which entered the museum's collection [fig. 3]. Also in 1961, he received a Fulbright grant to study at the Slade School of Art at the University of London from 1961 to 1963.

Barnes's advisor in London was Sir William Coldstream, who asked Francis Bacon, then at the Royal Academy of Arts, to critique Barnes's work. Through Bacon, Barnes

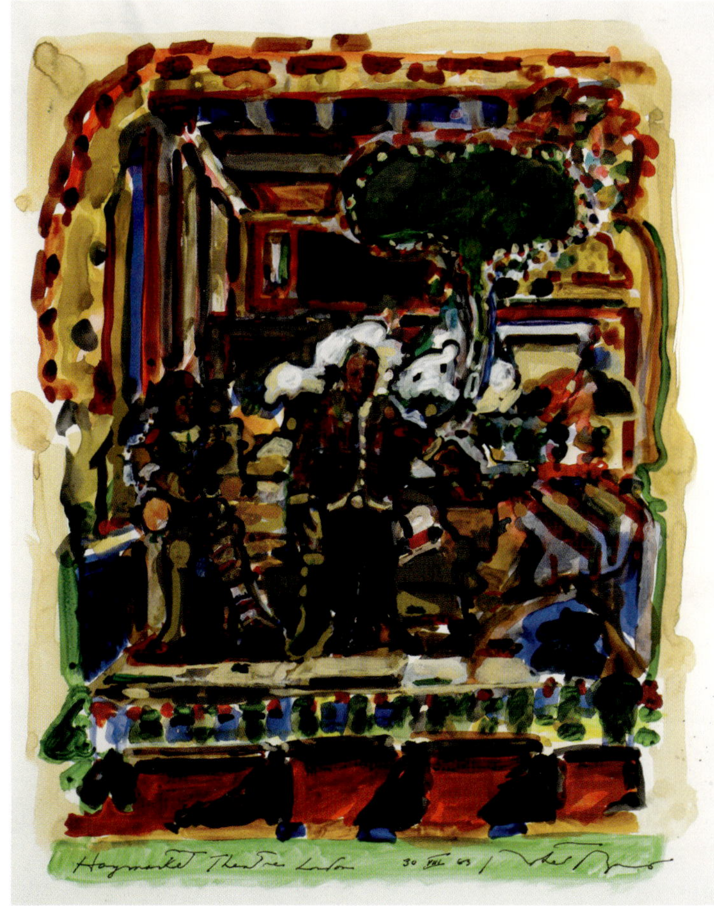

Fig. 4 Robert Barnes (American, b. 1934). **Haymarket Theater in London**, 1963. Watercolor and gouache on paper. The David and Alfred Smart Museum of Art, The University of Chicago, Gift of Dennis Adrian in honor of the artist, 2001.136. Photograph ©2015 courtesy of The David and Alfred Smart Museum of Art, The University of Chicago

discovered the London theater scene, rekindling his earlier interest, and he attended many famous venues such as Covent Garden, the Criterion, the Drury Lane, the Garrick, the Old Vic, the Royal Court, and the Haymarket, which is notable for being the first theater to use a "picture frame" proscenium, establishing an imaginary "fourth wall" [fig. 4]. From these experiences, Barnes produced a series of small casein paintings, which led to the recurring use of a proscenium as a framing device and the image of a stage-like platform as a form of spatial index. The London theater caseins also established serial imagery as a generative mode of production for Barnes.

Shortly after his return to the United States in 1963, Barnes began a tenure-track position at Indiana University, where his teaching, painting, and exhibiting established his independence from the mainstream currents at that time—minimalism and conceptualism—which disavowed painting as outmoded and irrelevant. Instead, Barnes's work of the late 1960s and 1970s anticipated the revitalization

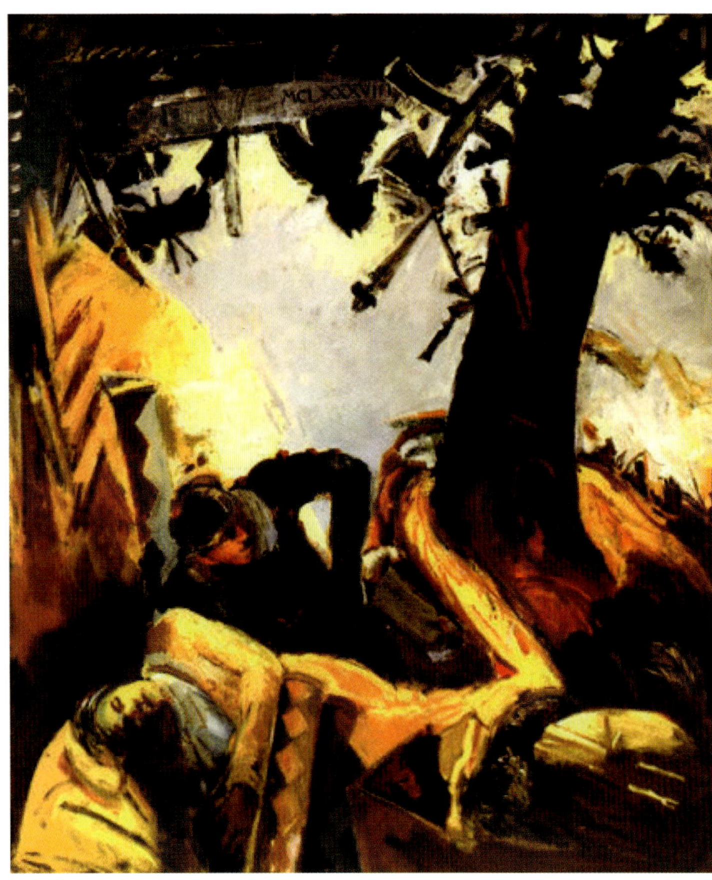

Fig. 5 Robert Barnes (American, born 1934). **The Cutting of the Elm,** 1992. Oil on canvas. Private collection, Chicago

of painting in Europe and the United States that was to accompany the rise of neo-expressionism in the late 1970s and 1980s, a movement that signaled a return to the mythic subject matter of figurative painting and the elevation of individualism, which the discipline of painting represents.

Perhaps in recognition of his prescience, Barnes was awarded the Childe Hassam purchase prize from the American Academy of Arts and Letters in 1970; a grant from the National Endowment for the Arts followed in 1982. This was followed by his 1985 mid-career survey organized by the Madison Art Center and a year-long sabbatical from IU, after which he returned to teaching in Bloomington as the Ruth N. Halls Professor of Fine Art. He retired in 1999 after thirty-five years as a driving force in Indiana University's School of Fine Arts and relocated to the remote coastal village of Searsport, Maine, in 2001.

Although the town of Searsport may strike no one as the ideal location for a painter to situate himself in the latter chapters of his career, Maine has a rich legacy of resident painters from Winslow Homer to John Marin to Marsden Hartley to Fairfield Porter and Alex Katz. Also, having produced fully one-tenth of deep-water ship captains in the nineteenth century (and hence attaining renown as "the home of the famous sea captains"), for Barnes, Searsport must echo with nautical lore and maritime superstitions, fueling his keen interest in works of literature about the sea (a criterion in Barnes's canon of literary works). In fact, Barnes's home in Searsport once belonged to one of the town's storied shipbuilders. It is the kind of place you might imagine Heinrich Heine's Flying Dutchman visiting in search of salvation, or where Ishmael bunked in the first chapter of *Moby Dick*.

Subjects since 1985

Up to the middle of the 1980s, Robert Barnes's subjects were characterized by the influence of literature and drama and the biographies of outcasts, artists, artistic eccentrics, poets, and writers. His subjects in subsequent decades are characterized by myth and legend, symbolism, cryptograms and the occult, the origins of mythology and religion, and autobiography. Evoking the "poesie" of Titian, Barnes's great Venetian touchstone who late in his career produced mythological paintings in domestic settings, Barnes's late work imagines the most quotidian aspects of life permeated by magical and supernatural forces and transformed into moments that are fateful, fantastic, and poetic.

His major painting cycles since the mid-1980s in large part have been informed by the writings of the Scottish anthropologist Sir James Frazer and the English poet and novelist Robert Graves. Frazer's monumental study in mythology and religion *The Golden Bough: A Study in Comparative Religion* (1890–1915) was groundbreaking and controversial in its comparison of Christianity with other world religions and myths. Robert Graves's study of mythopoetic inspiration *White Goddess: A Historical Grammar of Poetic Myth* (1948) was innovative in its speculative premise of the ancient worship of a single, prototypical goddess under many different names.[5] The poet's reinterpretation of classical Greek mythology in *The Greek Myths* (1955) has also been an important source of interpretive association for Barnes, but *The Golden Bough* and *The White Goddess* serve to bookend Barnes's archive of sources, encompassing ideas and interpretations that are universal and limitless in their application to the creative, transformative process and Barnes's visual language.

The fundamental concepts from these two books, which have provided multiple, interrelated themes and subjects for Barnes's paintings, are the ritualistic human sacrifice of a "sacred king" and Graves's White Goddess, based largely on Celtic mythology. Graves makes an argument for the existence of his prototypical goddess as the earliest, primal source of inspiration for artists and poets, citing ancient Ogham letters (known also as the "tree alphabet" of Gaelic Ireland and Britain) as ciphers dedicated to her. The universal themes of struggle, power, death, and transformation interwoven in these texts are told by Barnes through folklore and personal anecdote, and are directly linked to his daily practice in the solitude of his studio: the marshaling of forces (painting materials and their properties) and the resolution of an image on the surface of a painting, transforming the crude stuff of its origins into something symbolic. For that reason, their influence is significant in Barnes's work since 1985: they provide the thematic program for three major series, *The Sources of Power*, *Blood and Perfume*, and *The Ogham*.

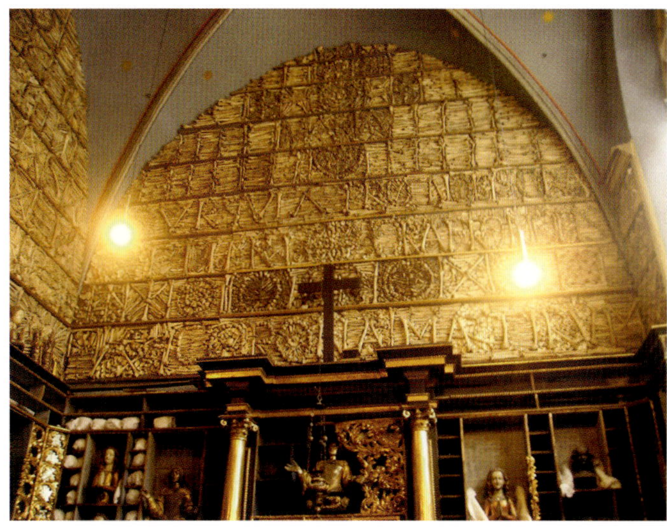

Fig. 6 Golden Chamber. Room of bones with relics. St. Ursula Church, Cologne, North Rhine-Westphalia, Germany.

In his series *The Sources of Power*, Barnes considers aspects of power including wisdom, beauty, sexuality, wealth, and physical strength. His painting *The Cutting of the Elm* (1992) [fig. 5] refers to an incident in 1188 during peace negotiations between Philip II of France and Henry II of England at Gisors, France. Henry and his army occupied the only shade on the field, beneath a huge elm, during a hot summer day. Ironically, in the midst of the truce, a battle broke out for possession of the tree. When the French attempted to destroy the elm, the English reinforced its trunk with bands of steel. The battle was won when Philip's men cut down the tree. In *The Cutting of the Elm*, the tree is besieged by weapons and is shown in the process of being felled. A blood red slash of color signals the terminal cut at the base of the trunk around which lie casualties of the skirmish.

The Cutting of the Elm represents physical power and also alludes obliquely to Frazer's *Golden Bough* tale of the sacrificial killing of the king. As a mock castration, a bough is broken from the sacred oak tree around which the king keeps vigil. It is the weapon used by the new king to kill the old. Emerging from a symbolic opening, after passing through "the world of the dead," the king may begin to reign anew. Frazer interprets the ritual death of the Sacred King as a custom representing renewal and regeneration. He describes the King of the Wood at Nemi (where the sacrifice was born) as an incarnation of the tree spirit.[6] Graves also describes a midsummer ritual sacrifice of the sacred oak king in *The White Goddess*.

Barnes followed *The Sources of Power* in 1996 with *Blood and Perfume*, an enigmatic series that explores a different category of power, based on the olfactory sense and various chapters of history related to perfumes and perfumers. In this series, which is the most broadly represented in the exhibition, Barnes infuses obscure accounts of the mystical and supernatural with the memory-inducing power of fragrance. Perhaps more important to Barnes, though, is the allegorical richness of perfume, especially as an analogy for painting: like pigment, oil, and turpentine, the ingredients of perfume such as musk or ambergris are pungent and unpleasant in their raw forms. But they are transformed into something rare, elusive, delightful, and arousing, like art, when processed in the manufacture of perfume. Oil painting is an olfactory experience in and of itself, so as an experiment, Barnes mixed perfume with his paint while working on the series to trigger imagery through the combined scents of paint, turpentine, and perfume.

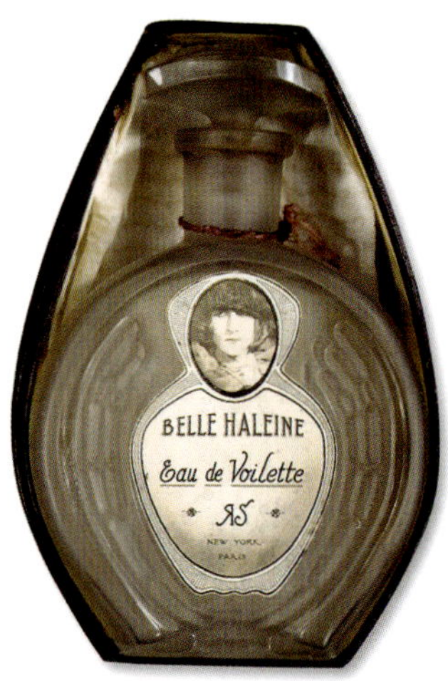

Fig. 7 Marcel Duchamp (French, 1887–1968) and Man Ray (American, 1890–1976). **Belle Haleine, Eau de Violette**, 1921. Assisted Readymade: perfume bottle with collage. ©Man Ray Trust/ Artists Rights Society (ARS), NY/ADAGP, Paris 2015. Image ©Man Ray Trust/ADAGP-ARS/Telimage–2015

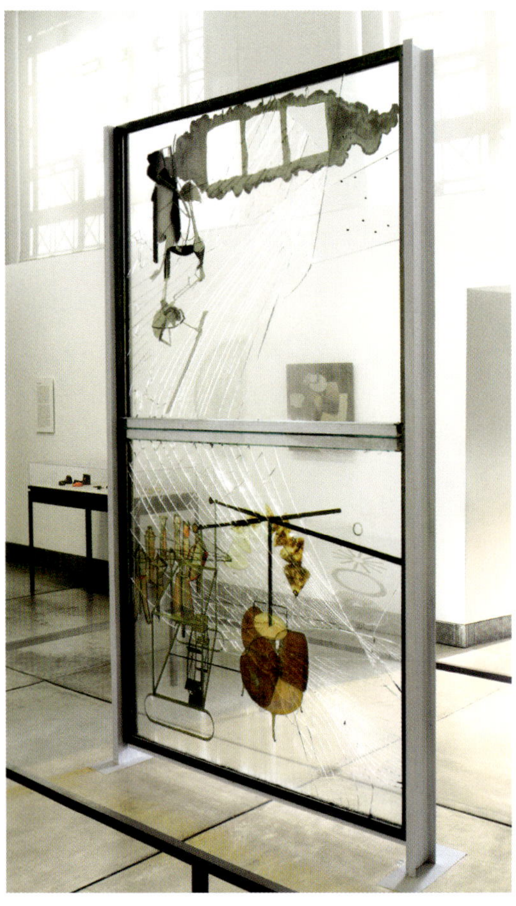

Fig. 8 Marcel Duchamp (French, 1887–1968). **The Bride Stripped Bare by Her Bachelors, Even (The Large Glass)**, 1915–23. Oil, varnish, lead foil, lead wire, and dust on two glass panels. Philadelphia Museum of Art, Bequest of Katherine S. Dreier, 1952 ©Succession Marcel Duchamp/ADAGP, Paris/Artists Rights Society (ARS), New York 2015. Photograph and digital image ©Philadelphia Museum of Art

The series also provided Barnes an opportunity to revisit Melville's *Moby Dick*, reflecting upon the irony of perfume's abject ingredients:

> Now that the incorruption of this most
> fragrant ambergris should
> be found in the heart of such decay; is this
> nothing? … Also
> forget not the strange fact that of all things
> of ill- savor, Cologne-water, in its rudimental
> manufacturing stages, is the worst.[7]

The subject of *Ursula—Cologne* (1996; plate 10) is the tomb of St. Ursula, the legendary leader of eleven thousand virgins all of whom were reputedly martyred in Cologne by the Huns in the fourth century AD. As legend has it, when the mass grave of St. Ursula and the virgins was uncovered in 1150, a stench filled the air, but this was replaced by the smell of flowers as soon as a horse's jawbone, which was buried with the remains, was removed— the "odor of sanctity" proved the martyrs' divinity. The upper register of the painting includes suggestions of skulls and the zigzag patterns of bones that cover the walls of the Golden Chamber in the Basilica of St. Ursula in Cologne [fig. 6]. The figure silhouetted at the center of the composition seems either to be plumbing the depths of the tomb or drawing something out from it, perhaps the horse's jawbone, which lies next to him in the foreground. An arc of greenish blue suggests the vaporous unmasking of the flowery scent of the virgins' remains after the malodorous object was removed.

Ursula and her entourage of virgins are equivalents for Graves's White Goddess in her manifold forms. Their martyrdom fixed their place as sanctified beings in the heavenly firmament and inspired a cult that was widespread in medieval Europe, like the cult of the White Goddess in the pre-Christian era.

Also from the *Blood and Perfume* series, *Belle Haleine, eau de Violette* (1996; plate 7) pays homage to Marcel Duchamp, with whom Barnes shared a friendship until Duchamp's death in1968. Duchamp's female alter-ego Rrose Sélavy is featured in the lower right, based on the famous photograph by Man Ray (1920–21), as well as near the top center portion of the painting, based on the label of *Belle Haleine, Eau de Violette*, an assisted ready made by Duchamp and Man Ray

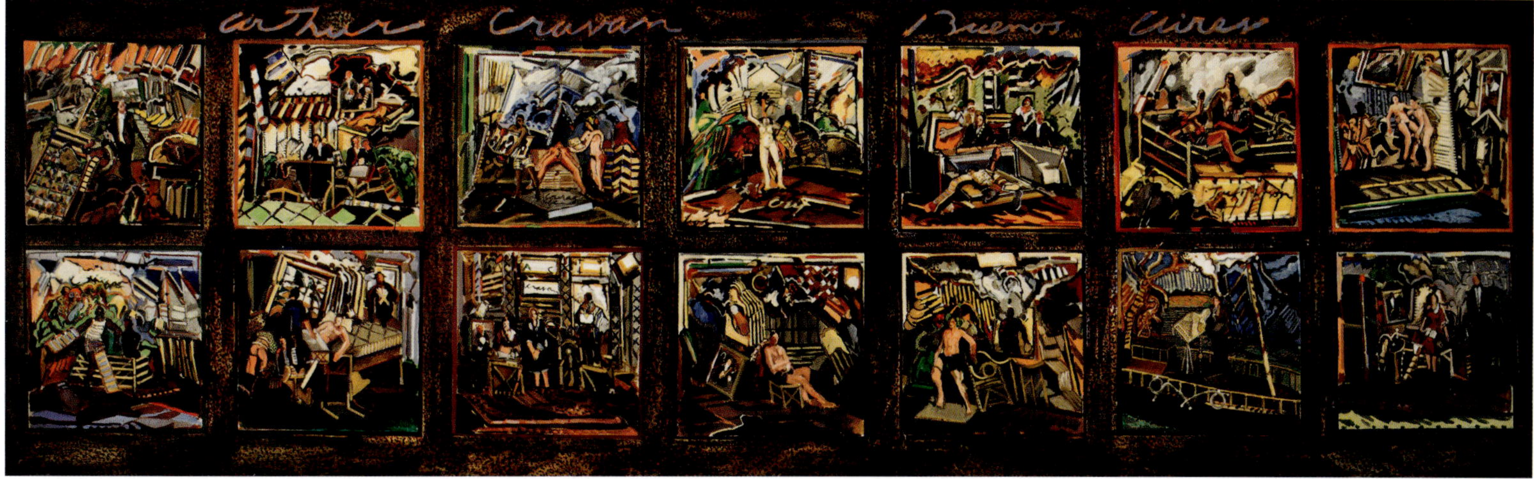

Fig. 9 Robert Barnes (American, b. 1934). **Arthur Cravan Still Lives**, 1968. Oil on canvas. The David and Alfred Smart Museum of Art, The University of Chicago; Gift of Dennis Adrian in honor of the artist and Lolli Thurm, 2005.69. Photograph ©2015, courtesy of the David and Alfred Smart Museum of Art, The University of Chicago

in the form of a perfume bottle [fig. 7]. Duchamp's gender-bending counterpart might just as well represent another manifestation of the White Goddess, whose spirit is released from a perfume bottle labeled "beautiful breath, veil water" recalling the florid scent released by Ursula's divine remains. Prominently, Duchamp's "ectoplasmic thought cloud" from *The Large Glass* also appears in the top register of the painting [fig. 8]. Besides the metanarrative of *The Large Glass* related to cycles of love, desire, suffering and sexual unfulfillment, its three-part storyboard in the upper portion was an early source for Barnes's large sequential painting *Arthur Cravan Still Lives*, which is an outlying but important variation on his longstanding practice of producing serial imagery [fig. 9].

Barnes's *Ogham* series also alludes to Robert Graves's *White Goddess*, proposing that the ancient Ogham alphabet is a cipher related to customs of Graves's prototypical White Goddess in all her various forms. The Ogham is known as the "tree alphabet" because the names of various trees and their attributes, including fragrances, were associated by medieval Irish poets with individual letters. Graves suggested that ancient people of the Aegean, whom he called "the sea people," passed on their knowledge of the goddess to the ancient poets of Ireland and Wales through the hermetic Ogham alphabet.

In *Hawthorn* (2000; plate 16), a thorny thicket divides the canvas in half, the upper portion representing the realm of the living and the lower portion that of the dead. Hunters in the foreground are pursuing their prey, a fox concealed beneath the cover of the hawthorn hedgerow. Protected by the dense bramble are stones or skulls and the indication of a coffin protruding into the lower left corner of the painting— images of death that may refer to the putrid odor that some hawthorn varieties emit. The fragrance attributed to each tree in Barnes's *Ogham* series provides an associative bridge between it and the *Blood and Perfume* series.

The Sea

Several paintings in *Grand Allusions* are related to Barnes's enduring fascination with the sea, maritime lore, and Celtic mythology—themes that have become more prominent in his late career. The sea personified is like a femme fatale for Barnes, recognizing as he does that "there's something about the sea that beckons you lovingly, and then you know it'll kill you." In his North Sea paintings, Barnes reflects on maritime lore and folk legends of Scotland and Ireland, imagining the sea's awesome power, unfathomable depths, and the mysteries that might lie beneath the cresting swells of its dangerous waves. The mythological silkie is Barnes's personification of the sea. Silkies are seal-like creatures of the underworld in Scottish lore who have the power to become human upon shedding their skin in order to satisfy romantic or sexual desires on land. They embody themes of poetic transformation, transfiguration, and renewal in Barnes's work of the late 1980s and 90s.

The silkie emerges from her skin as a human being in the foreground of *Silkie* (1989; plate 3) only to return to the sea in the middle distance, representing for Barnes the evanescent nature of artistic inspiration. The pictorial space, emphasized by Barnes's characteristically dramatic

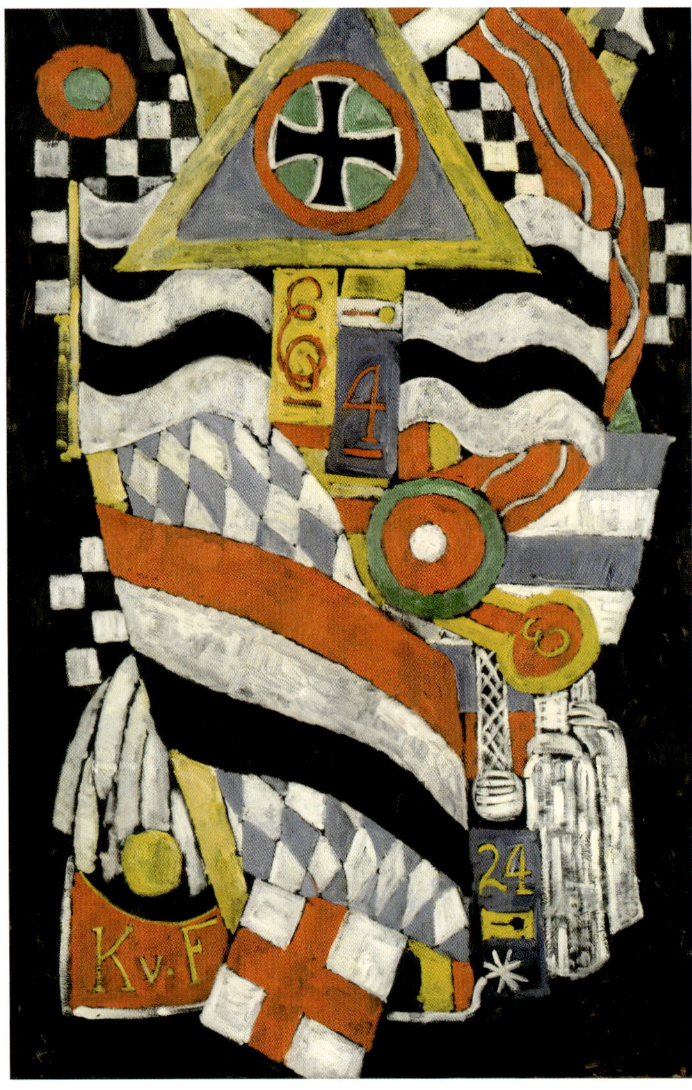

Fig. 10 Marsden Hartley (American, 1877–1943). **Portrait of a German Officer**, 1914. Oil on canvas. The Metropolitan Museum of Art, Alfred Stieglitz Collection, 1949, 49.70.42. Image copyright ©The Metropolitan Museum of Art; image source: Art Resource, NY

chiaroscuro, collapses into almost complete abstraction in the upper portion of the painting in a bedlam of forms that recalls the flat yet vitally expressive and symbolic pictorial fields of Marsden Hartley's German officer paintings of 1914 [fig. 10]. In Barnes's painting the silkie presides over the unruly sea, which is an arena for the collision of metaphysical forces, human vulnerability, and nature.

The Maine sea coast, the subject of Barnes's work since 2001, has been the setting for histories and anecdotes related to his life in Maine, while evoking myths and legends with universal meanings. In *Choppy Seas Out of Carver's Slip* (2001; plate 19) a boat full of fishermen navigates the breakers off the island of Vinalhaven. The prow of their vessel seems to be riding the luminous crest of a wave, which divides the composition into upper and lower realms—that of the fishermen and their daily, if perilous, routine, and an imaginary realm beneath the waves which opens onto colorful and fantastic images of the suboceanic spirit world. Similarly, in *The Mackerel Run—Belfast Harbor* (2002; plate 20), the composition is divided into upper and lower registers in which fisherman are casting off the side of a bridge, beneath which steams a mysterious ship ferrying a shadowy, knife-wielding figure and surrounded by varieties of marks that suggest, alternately, a starry night or an expanse of bioluminescent forms. And in *Sears Island* (2002; plate 18) shell fisherman are at work in the shallows of the island's west shore. The evening setting provides the conditions for a tenebrous, dream-like image, which transforms the scene of fishermen at work into an image of the netherworld, representing the seaman's realm of the dead, Davy Jones's Locker.

Self-Portrait Vanitas (plate 21), also from 2002, shows Barnes in an embrace with the skeletal image of death, recalling Arnold Böcklin's *Self-Portrait with Death Playing the Fiddle* (1872) [fig. 11]. In Böcklin's painting, Death plays a violin over the artist's shoulder as the artist pauses, suspending his loaded brush in consideration of his own image on the canvas. Barnes also depicts himself in a moment of reflection, literally and figuratively, as he looks at the mirror from which he is working. Here, the bony hand of death holds the brush, not the artist. Behind Barnes on the wall is a convex mirror reflecting the studio, a symbol of vanitas reflecting the decay and decline of the material world over the course of time.

As a vanitas, Barnes's painting presents adumbrations of death cast over the span of his career, concisely summarized in the painting from the architecturally compartmentalized space of the bottom portion, recalling his work of the 1960s, to shadowy images of the daemon from paintings of the 1980s on the back wall, to references to the Ogham tree alphabet and allusions to Frazer's ritual killing of the king in his series of the 1990s. Barnes's *Vanitas* is a meditation on the arc of a long, prolific career, and the inevitability of death's victory over the metaphorical struggle that painting represents.

Barnes's marshaling of forces in the studio for the past sixty years—intellectual, physical, and psychic—always has been about awakening the creative spirit to grapple with the ever-present reality of the end and its inevitability. Returning to the solitude of the studio every day, Barnes has always embodied the figure of Frazer's sacred, dying king, returning to the place where creative ceremonies and practices are played out in the cyclical course of his command of painting. The end of a painting signals the fulfillment of a physical and mental process, from which the artist withdraws and regenerates, beginning the cycle anew, assembling resources and mobilizing power in the service of his own muse-gods and goddesses in the guise of the multifarious artistic personages, personalities, and characters who populate his work and over whom the shadowy figure of death asserts his sovereignty in both the end and at the beginning of each poetic, artistic cycle.

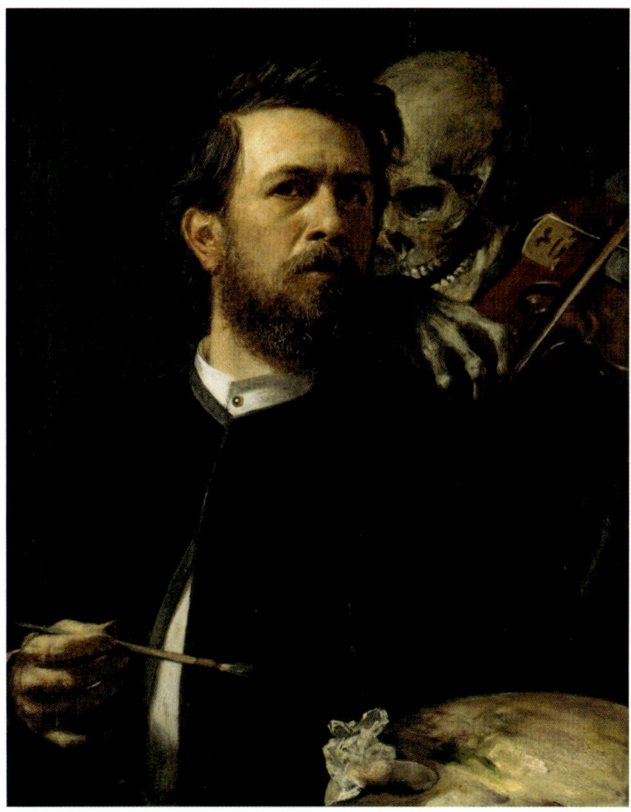

Fig. 11 Arnold Böcklin (Swiss-German, 1827–1901). **Self-Portrait with Death Playing the Fiddle**, 1872. Oil on canvas. Nationalgalerie, Staatliche Museen, Berlin, Germany. Photo: bpk, Berlin/Nationalgalerie, Staatliche Museen/Joerg P. Anders/Art Resource, NY

Notes

1. North worked as an editor of *Poetry Magazine* in the 1930s and 1940s. Barnes had played the part of Dr. Relling in a class production of Henrik Ibsen's *Wild Duck*. The Goodman School of Drama was affiliated with SAIC until 1978.

2. Barnes saw *Excavation* as a student after it was acquired by the Art Institute in 1954.

3. Levy was one of the first art dealers to introduce the work of Joseph Cornell and he also exhibited the work of Salvador Dali, Giorgio De Chirico, Max Ernst, Frida Kahlo, Mina Loy, René Magritte, Roberto Matta, and Dorothea Tanning, among many others in his Madison Avenue gallery between 1931 and 1942, and in his East 57th Street gallery between 1942 and 1949.

4. See Sir James George Frazer, *The Golden Bough*. Vol.1 (New York and London: Macmillan, 1894). Project Gutenberg. See also Robert Graves, *The White Goddess: A Historical Grammar of Poetic Myth*. New ed. (Manchester: Carcanet, 1997).

5. Frazer, ibid, 240–53. Project Gutenberg. (Web, 13 December 2014).

6. Herman Melville, *Moby Dick*, in *The Writings of Herman Melville*, 2nd ed (Evanston, IL and Chicago: Northwestern University Press and The Newberry Library,1991), 409.

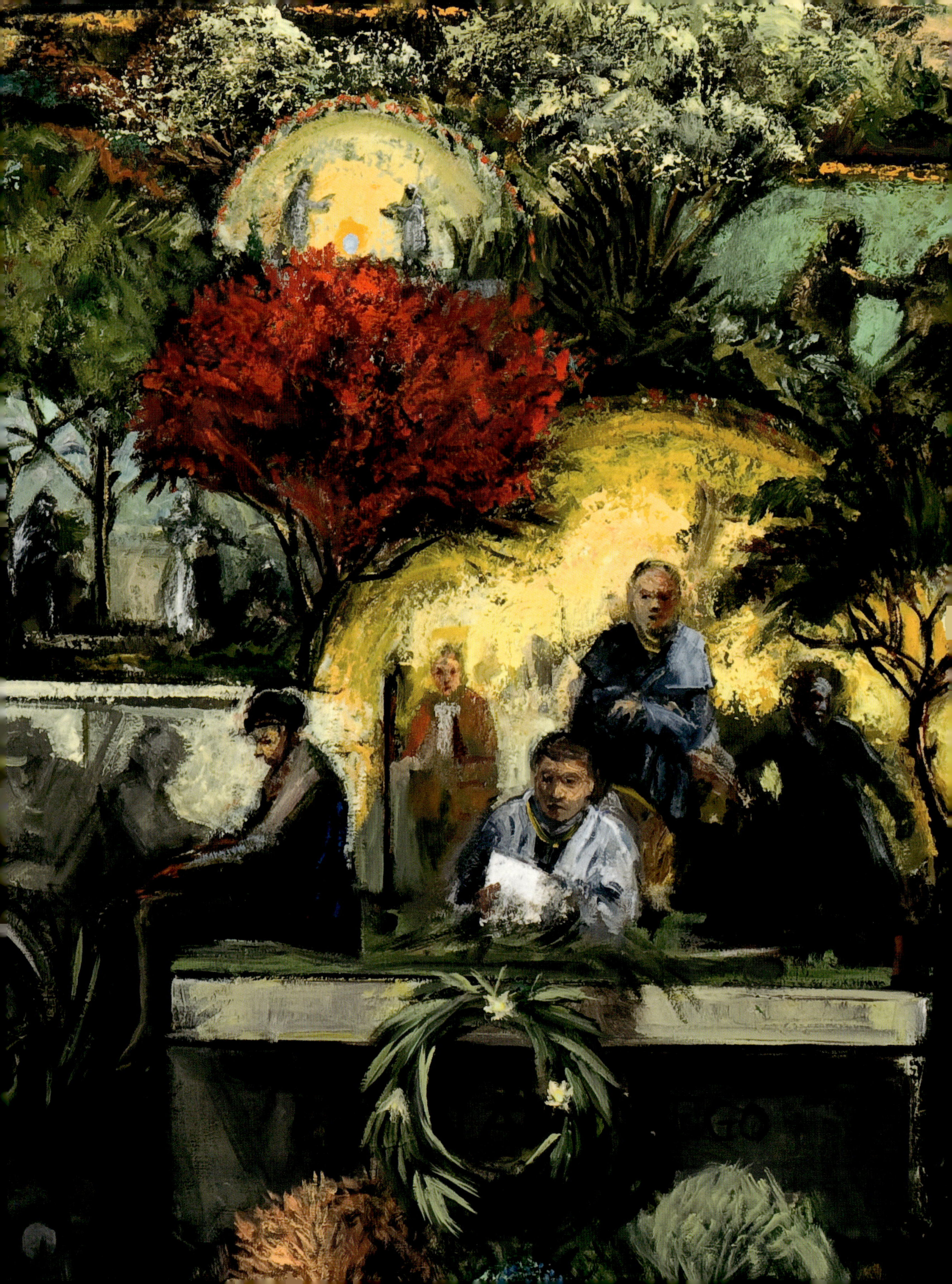

CATALOGUE

NANETTE ESSECK BREWER

NOTES TO THE PLATES

Measurements are given for canvas, panel, or sheet.
Height precedes width; measurements are given in inches, then centimeters.

PLATE 1

Danaë, 1985
Oil on canvas
60 x 55 ¼ (152.4 x 140.3)
Courtesy of the artist and Corbett vs. Dempsey Gallery, Chicago

This painting depicts a famous episode from the Greek myth of Danaë, the daughter of King Acrisius of Argos. After an oracle foretells his death at the hands of his daughter's son, the king imprisons Danaë in a fortress to keep her chaste. This mortal's ploy, however, is no match for the god Jupiter, who magically impregnates the young virgin through a shower of gold. Unlike more traditional representations, the narrative's main character is shown upside down and relegated to the lower-right corner of the picture. In contrast to this miraculous conception, an earthly couple engages in carnal activities on the upper left.

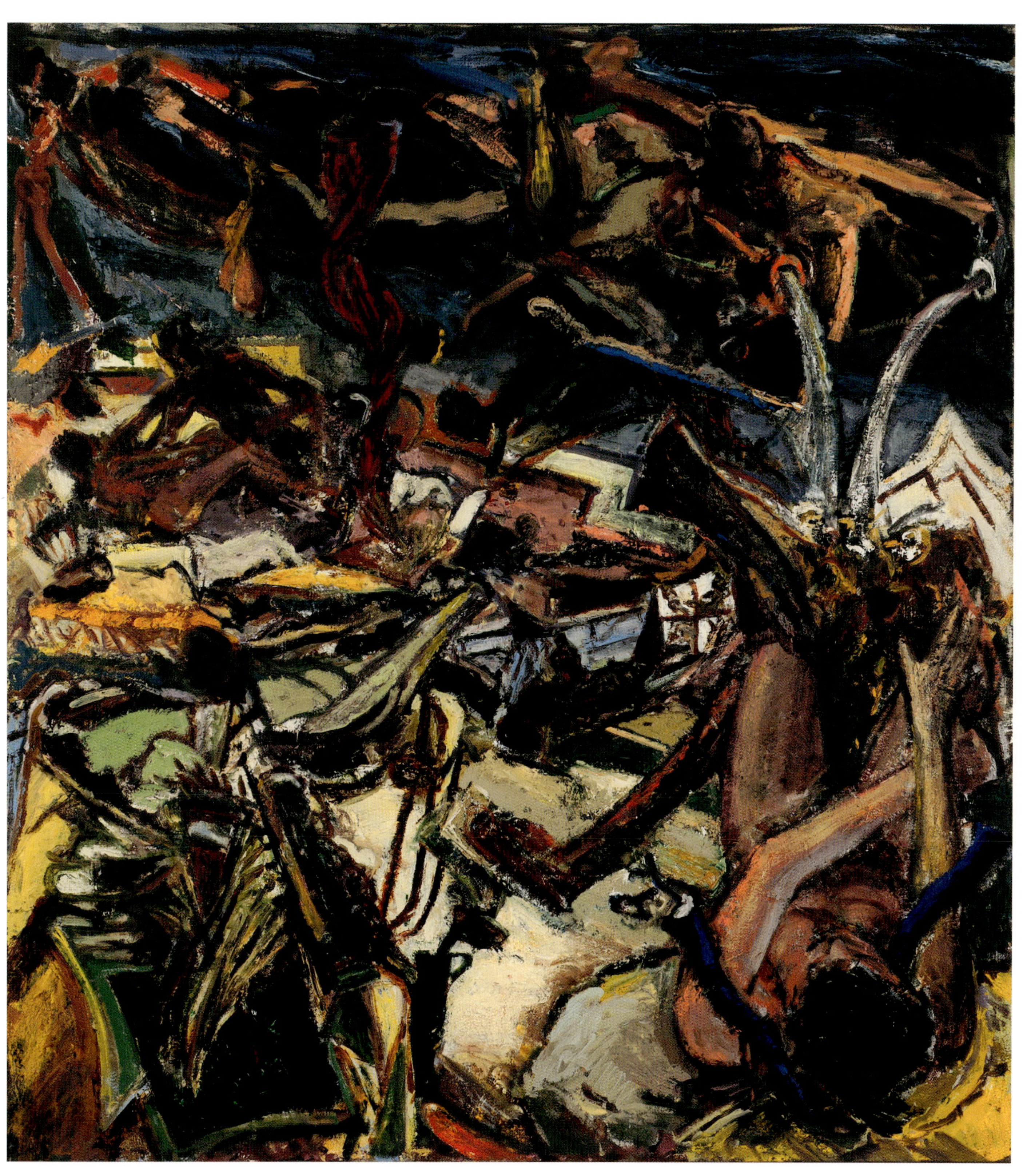

PLATE 2

Quiet History, 1986
Oil on canvas
87 ¼ x 51 ¼ (221.6 x 130.2)
Collection of The Art Institute of Chicago, Twentieth-Century Discretionary, Twentieth-Century Purchase, Oscar L. Gerber Memorial, and A. James Speyer funds; restricted gifts of Dr. and Mrs. Orrin M. Scheff and Mr. and Mrs. Lawrence Aronson, 1987.140

This vertical, zigzagging composition is anchored in the lower left corner by a solitary seated male figure, a scholar-historian who quietly contemplates the view before him. Although subtle references to classical sculpture, such as the standing white form in the upper right, allude to the history of Western art, they are not meant to recall a specific time and place, but rather to evoke the passage of time. The observer is both enthralled by the vast treasures spread before him, but also overwhelmed and, perhaps, humbled by their presence.

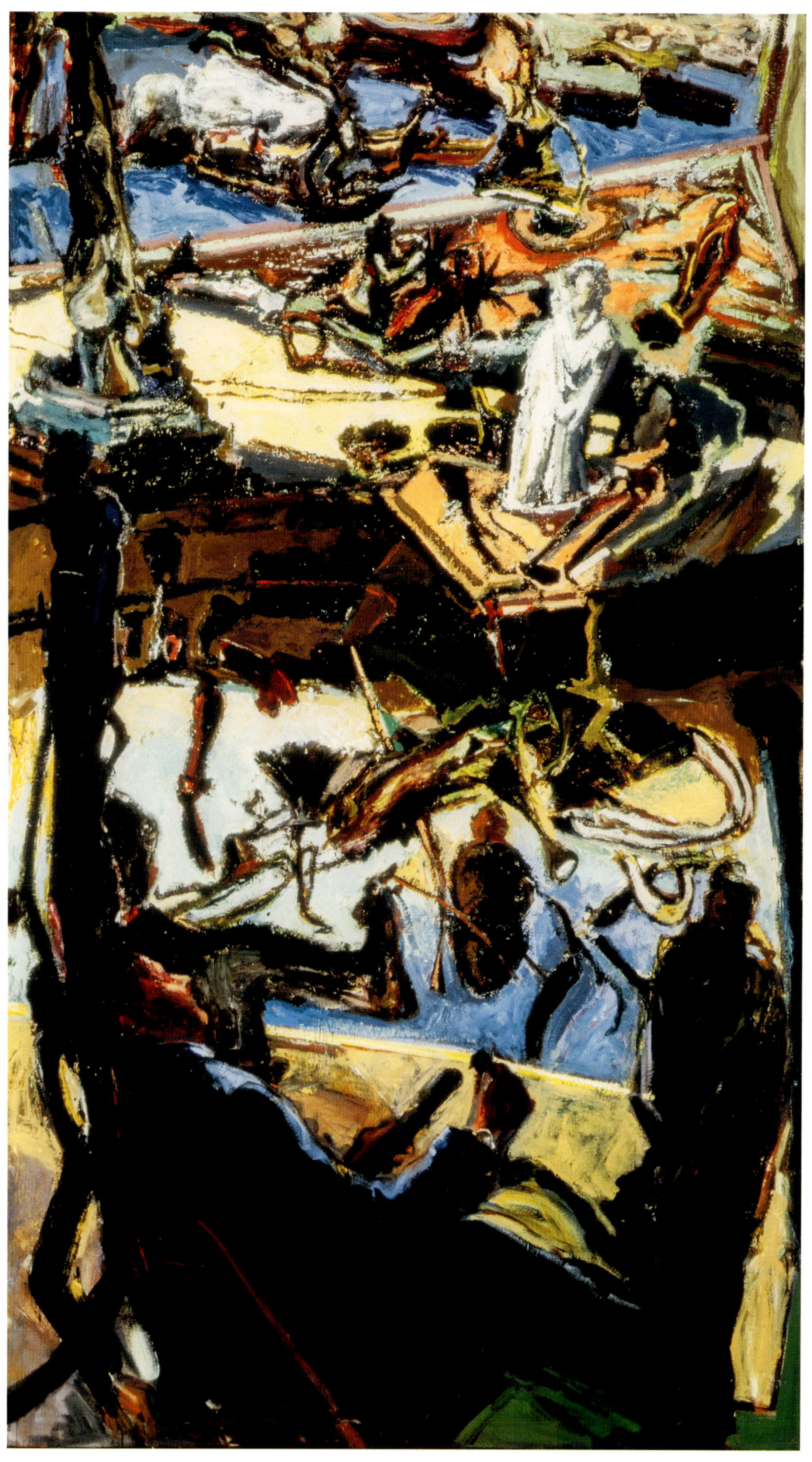

PLATE 3

Silkie, 1987
Series: Silkies
Oil on canvas
78 ¾ x 88 (200 x 223.5)
Collection of the Indianapolis Museum of Art, Henry F. and
Katherine D. DeBoest Memorial Fund, 1989.1

One of two Silkie canvases, this loosely painted image draws its inspiration from an old Scottish myth by way of a folk song, "The Grey Silkie," sung by Jean Redpath in 1975. In the story a male silkie (half man/half seal) mates with a human and then abandons her to return to the sea. The silkie comes back seven years later to claim his son. The woman's new husband, a harpoon gunner, tracks them down and kills both in revenge. While the painting refrains from a literal depiction, hints of the narrative appear in the nude female figure emerging from a dark seal skin, alluding to their tragic union; the boat of the hunter appears beneath a pink curtain near the center of the composition.

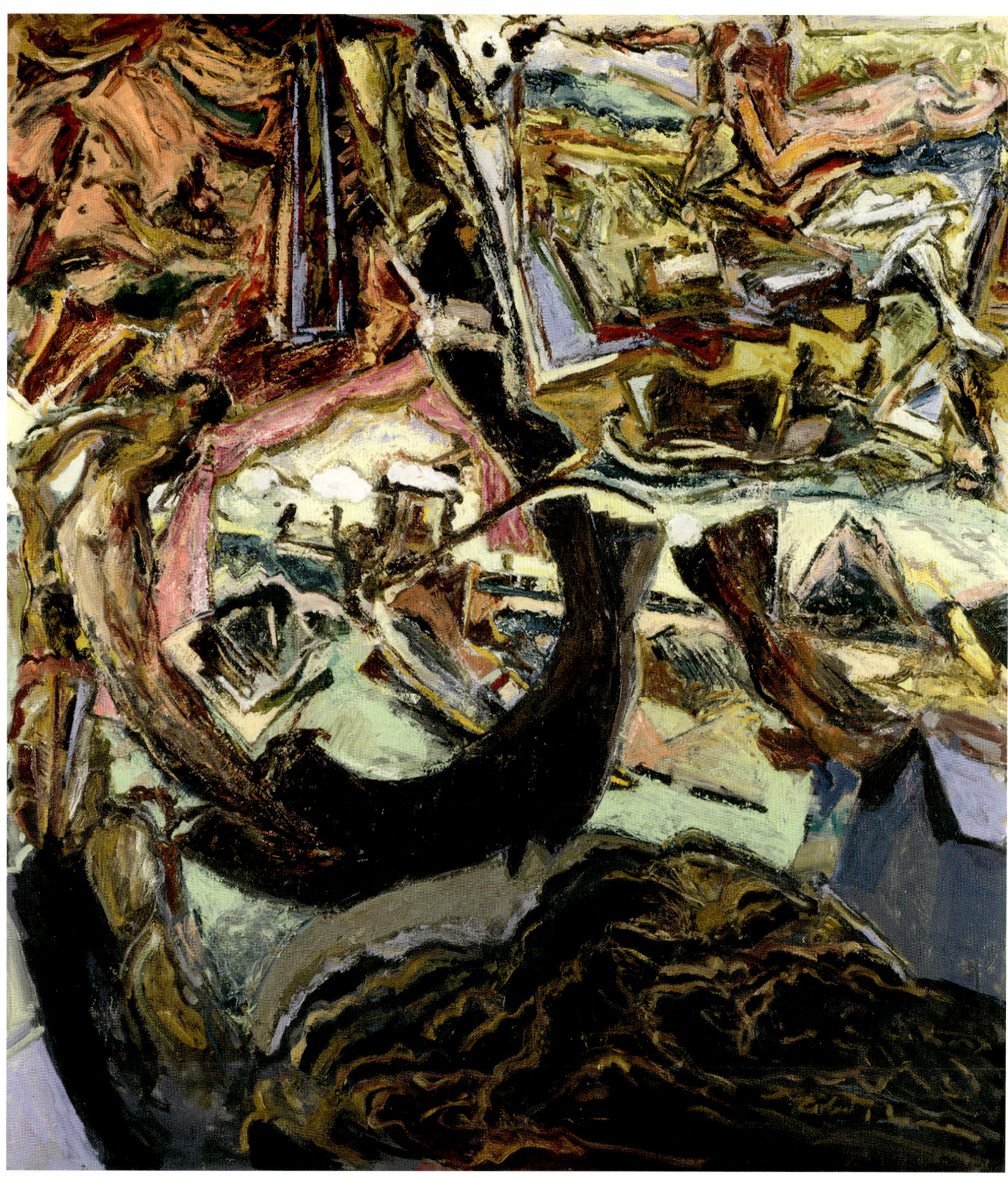

PLATE 4

Finn McCool and the Salmon of Knowledge, 1992
Series: The Sources of Power
Oil on canvas
74 1⁄16 x 71¾ (188.1 x 182.2)
Collection of Kenneth and Patricia Northcott

Based on a Celtic legend, this scene presents the hero Finn McCool (Fionn mac Cumhaill) as a young man. With his teacher Finegas, Finn has been trying to catch the Salmon of Knowledge (*bradán feasa*) for seven years. The first person to consume of its flesh will gain all of the wisdom of the world (the ultimate brain food!). When they finally hook the magic and immortal fish, Finegas tells his student to cook it on an outdoor spit, but not to eat it. When a drop of hot fish oil splatters on his thumb, Finn instinctively sucks it off, not realizing what he has done. In so doing, he acquires the Salmon's knowledge, and thus he is transformed from a naïve fool into a wise and powerful leader.

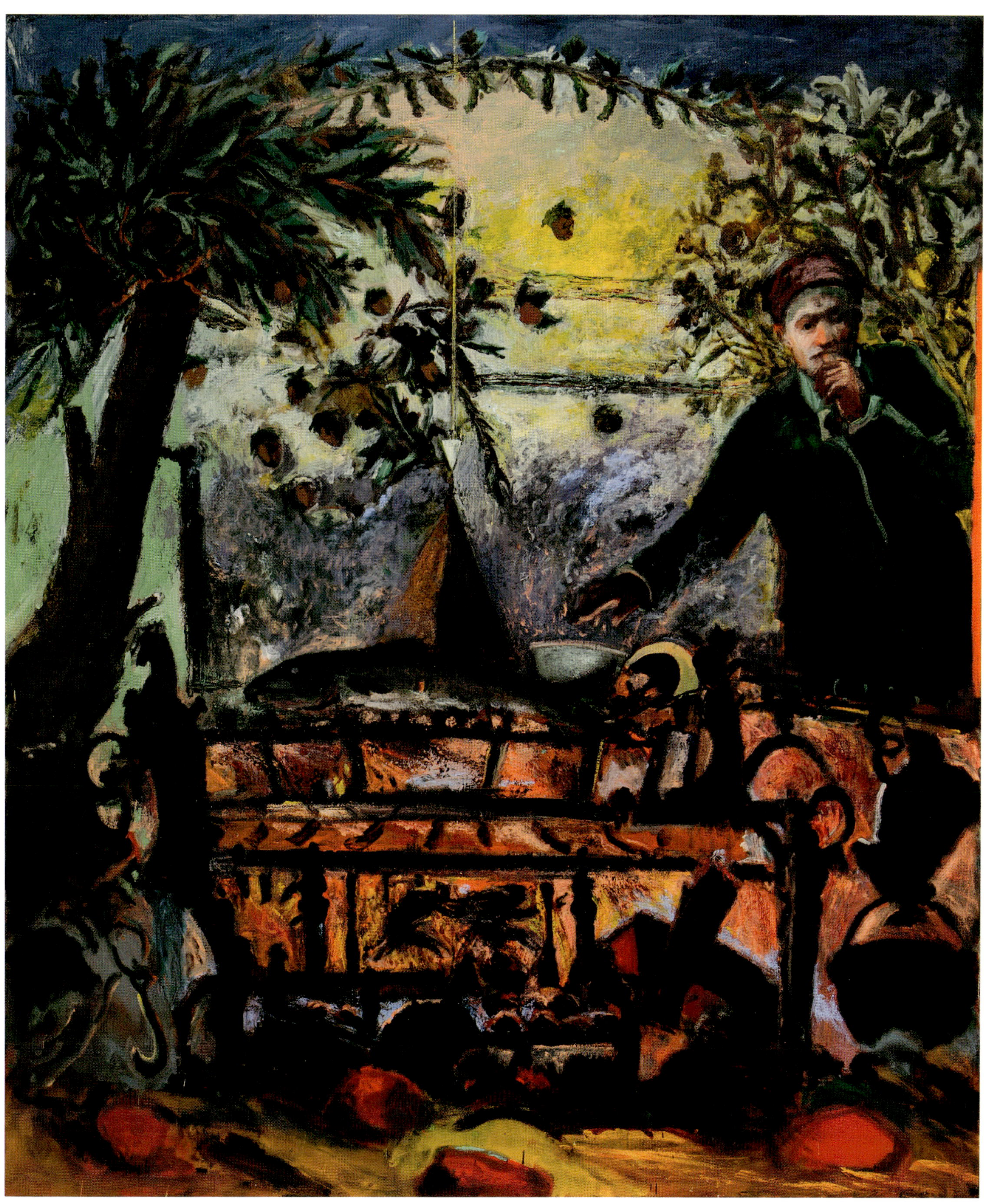

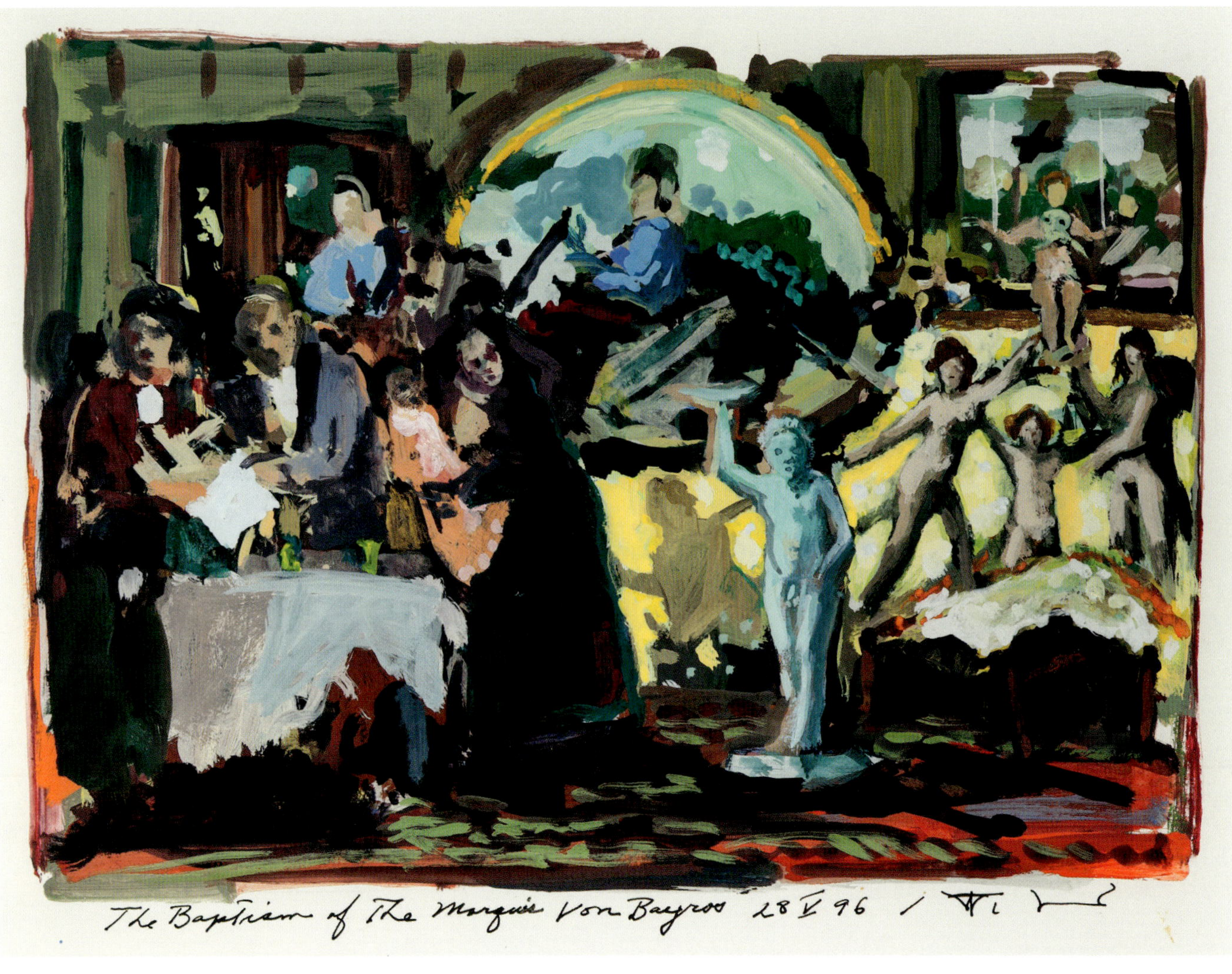

PLATE 5

The Baptism of the Marquis von Bayros, 1996
Casein on paper
13 $\frac{15}{16}$ x 17 (35.4 x 43.2)
Collection of Kenneth and Patricia Northcott

Intrigued by the life of Franz von Bayros—a late nineteenth-century Austrian painter and illustrator of the Decadent Movement known for his erotic series such as *Tales from the Dressing Table*—Barnes creates von Bayros's imaginary early biography. Born in Zagreb, Marquis von Bayros was raised in an aristocratic family as the son of an Austrian artist and a Spanish nobleman and eventually married the step-daughter of Johann Strauss II. The left-hand side of the composition shows him as a swaddled baby being introduced to the patrons of a brothel, while hints of his later pornographic work are indicated by the Eros statue and dancing nude sirens on the opposite side.

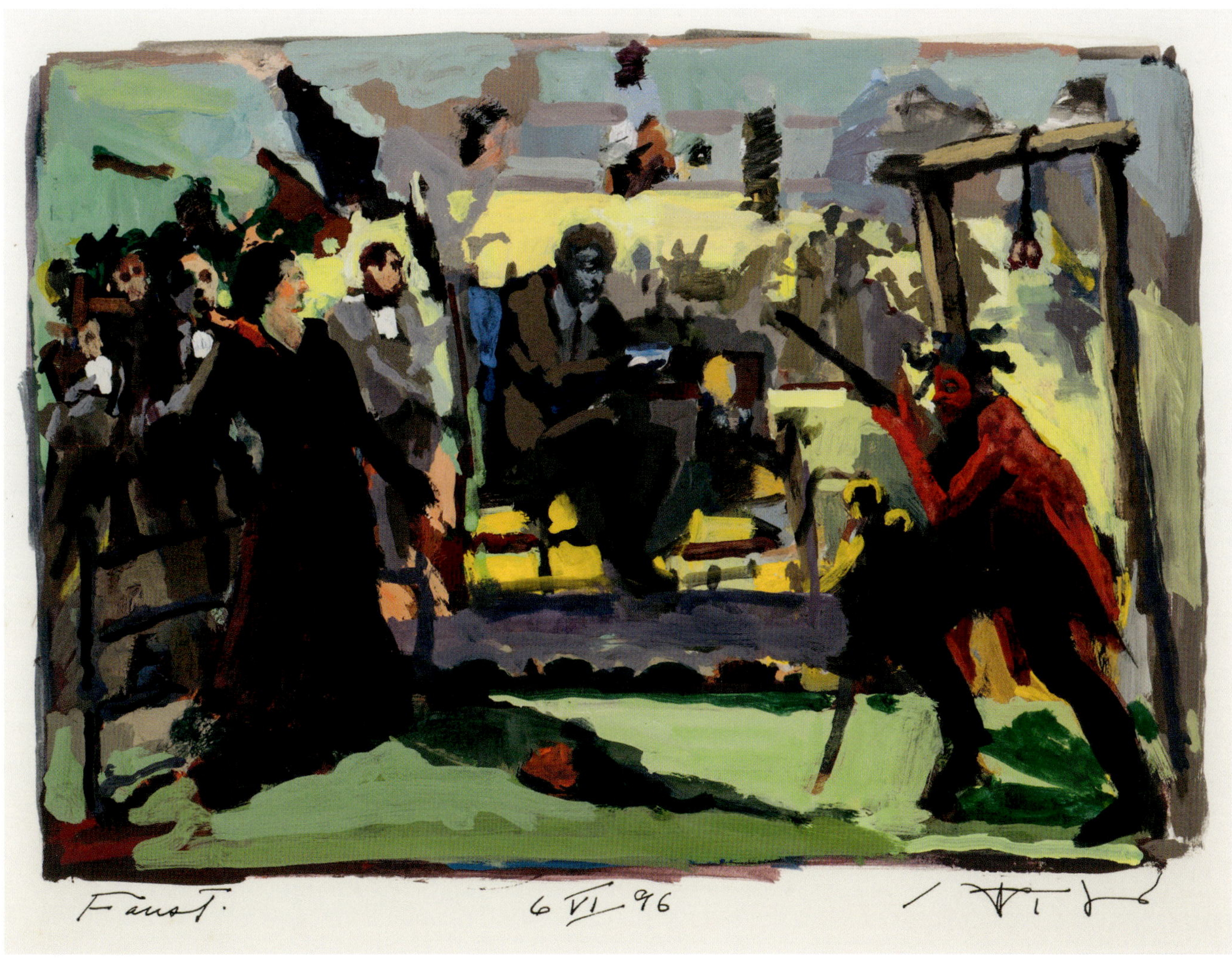

PLATE 6

Faust, 1996
Casein on paper
13 x 17 ½ (33 x 44.5)
Collection of the Estate of Ruth Horwich

Drawn to legends of doomed heroes striving for power, Barnes was naturally intrigued by Goethe's tale of Doctor Faust. In this scene, the depressed Faust is seated at the center of the composition, while a red devil (Mephistopheles), who makes a pact for his soul, points a gun at his head. As is often the case with such ambitious, vain men, there is a woman involved. Marguerite, Faust's lover, appears opposite the devil. As an indication of Faust's culpability in her tragic fate—the killing of her mother and their illegitimate child and ultimate sentence for murder—the noose on the gallows suggests a scrotum.

PLATE 7

Belle Haleine, eau de Violette, 1996
Series: Blood and Perfume
Oil on canvas
73 x 67 ½ (185.4 x 171.4)
Collection of the David and Alfred Smart Museum of Art, The University of Chicago; Purchase, Anonymous Gift 1997.101

The most Surrealist-inspired work of Barnes's later career, this painting borrows its title from Marcel Duchamp's assisted ready-made *Belle Haleine, Eau de Violette* (1921). Duchamp's sculpture was actually a bottle of perfume filled with the popular dime-store scent Evening in Paris, similar to the one depicted on a pedestal near the center of this composition. The bottle's altered label bore a photographic portrait of Duchamp dressed as Rrose Sélavy, his female alter ego, who looked similar to the hatted lady in the lower-right-hand corner of this image. Other references to Duchamp's artworks include the Cubist-like jumble that dominates the majority of the canvas and the three-paneled, cloud-like shape at the top, derived from Duchamp's *Large Glass*.

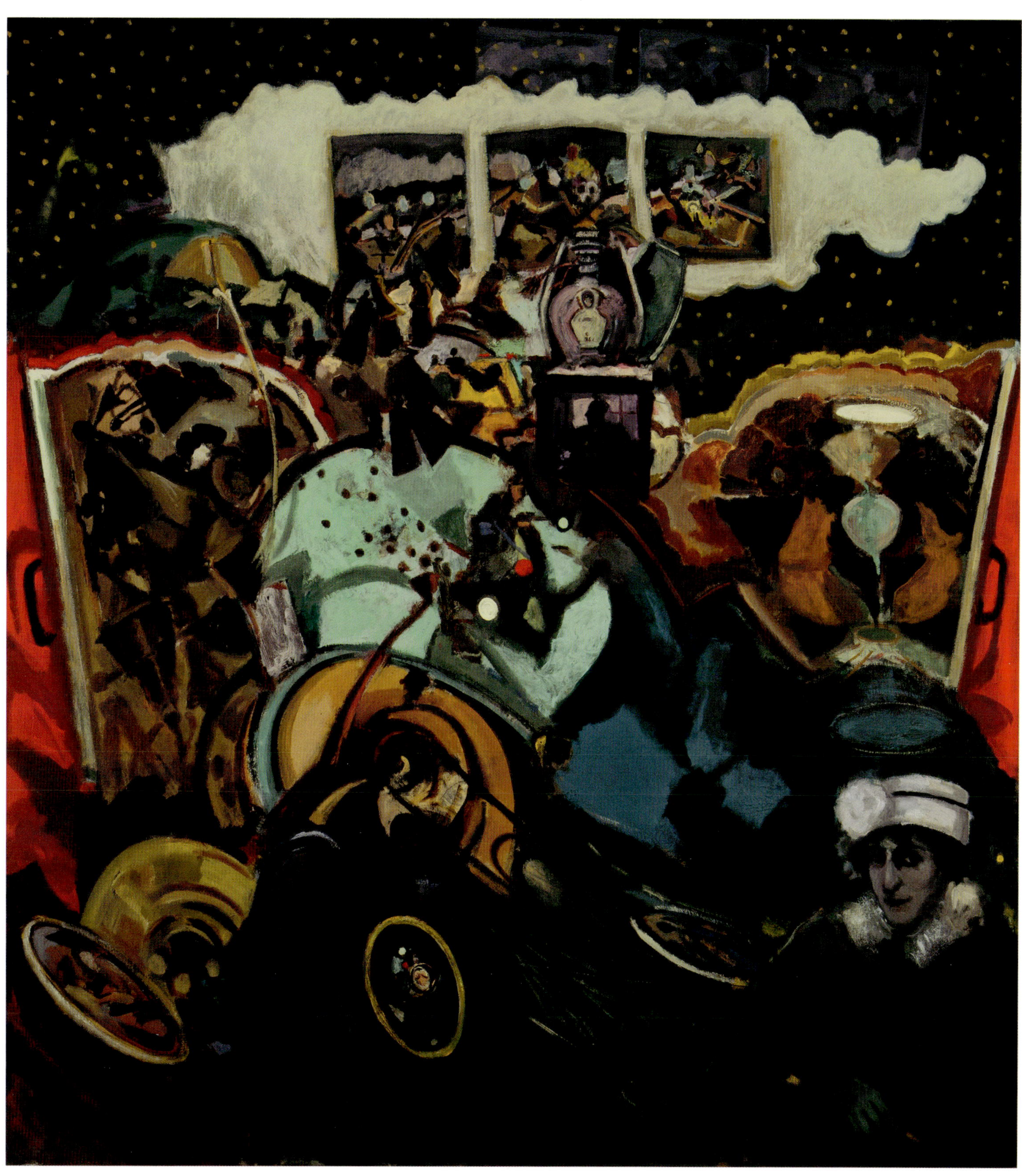

PLATE 8

Molinard-Grasse, 1996
Series: Blood and Perfume
Oil on canvas
72 x 72 ⅛ (182.9 x 183.2)
Collection of Lolli Thurm

The town of Grasse in the south of France is known as the perfume capital of the world. Founded in Grasse in 1849, the Maison Molinard helped to establish the modern French fragrance industry. On the right-hand side of this painting, the company's founder Monsieur Molinard conjures up an olfactory potion. All of ingredients in his imaginary factory magically fall into a cauldron to produce a heady eau de fleur (flower-scented water). The mirror on the floor reflects the light upwards to create eerie shadows on the figure's face and the wall. The artist himself reclines in the picture's shadowy lower register. The image's intense red color reflects the potency of Molinard's products, which also were used to add fragrance to cigarettes.

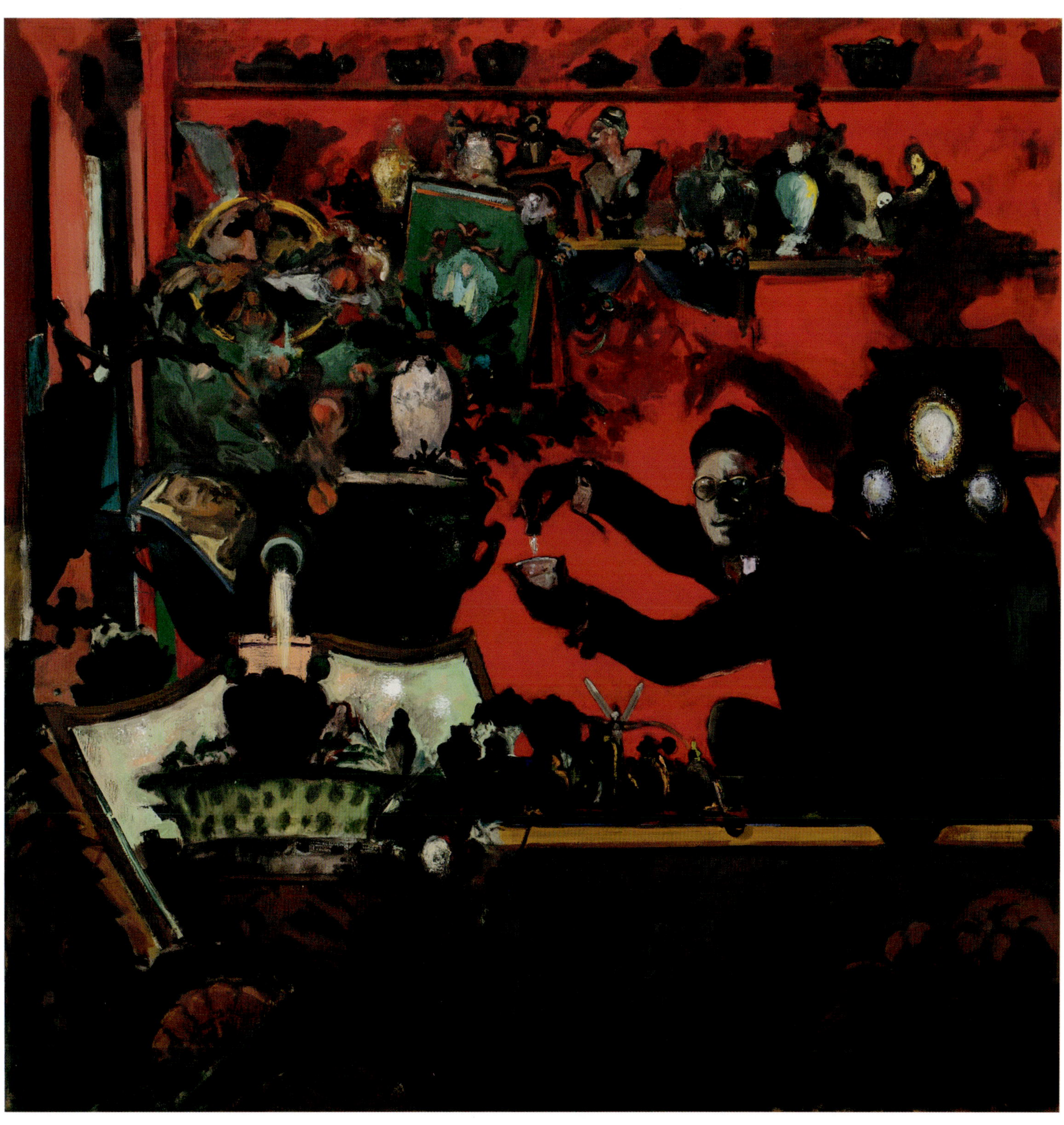

PLATE 9

Guerlain, 1996
Series: Blood and Perfume
Oil on canvas
73 x 67 (185.4 x 170.2)
Collection of David Sharpe and Anne Abrons

Pierre-François Pascal Guerlain, founder of one of the oldest perfume houses in Paris, wears an apron as he tests one of his concoctions in a glowing glass beaker. Guerlain's shop was a fashionable haunt of the city's high society. Among his clients were Empress Eugénie and Emperor Napoleon III (who named him as His Majesty's Official Perfumer), Queen Victoria of the United Kingdom, and Queen Isabella II of Spain. One of Guerlain's elegant glass bottles rests on the counter behind its creator, while the shop's purveyors are glimpsed in the background. On the left side of the painting, a young female customer (posed by the artist's daughter) seems entranced. The cloud-like forms suggest Guerlain's smoky fragrances as well as the mysterious power of scents to evoke the past.

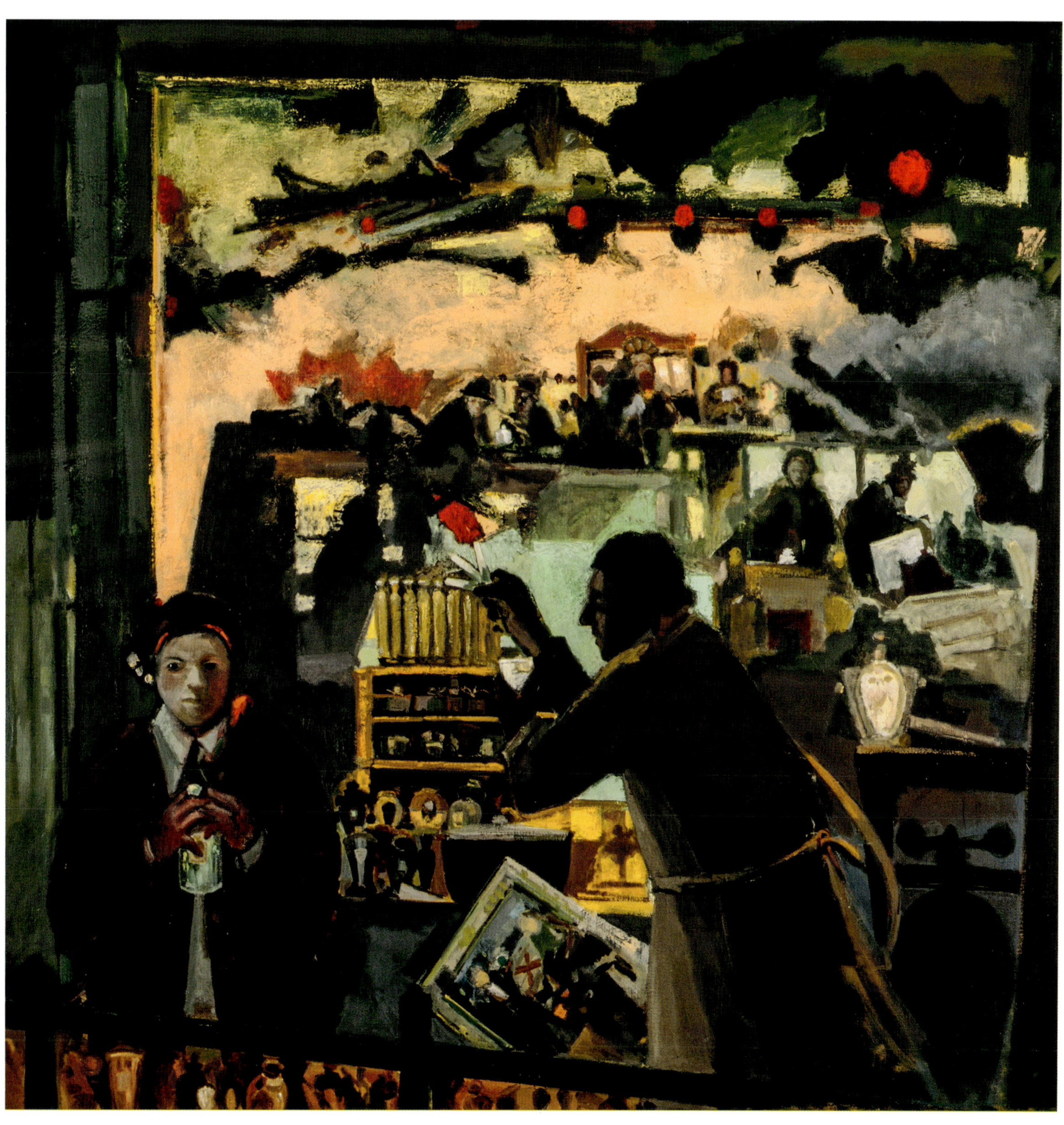

PLATE 10

Ursula—Cologne, 1996
Series: Blood and Perfume
61 x 77 ½ (155 x 196.9)
Collection of Jonas and Betsy Dovydenas

Barnes can't resist a pun in this image. Following the martyrdom of Saint Ursula, she was buried in Cologne Cathedral; eau de Cologne is a perfume originating in the German city in the eighteenth century. The circle in the center of the composition represents Ursula's open tomb, which gave off a terrible stench when uncovered. While the crowd on the right-hand side retreats in horror, a lone figure with a rope retrieves a horse's head (the skull-like death mask in the foreground). When this object is removed, the space fills with the sweet-smelling "odor of sanctity," a delicious aroma said to be given off by the remains of saints.

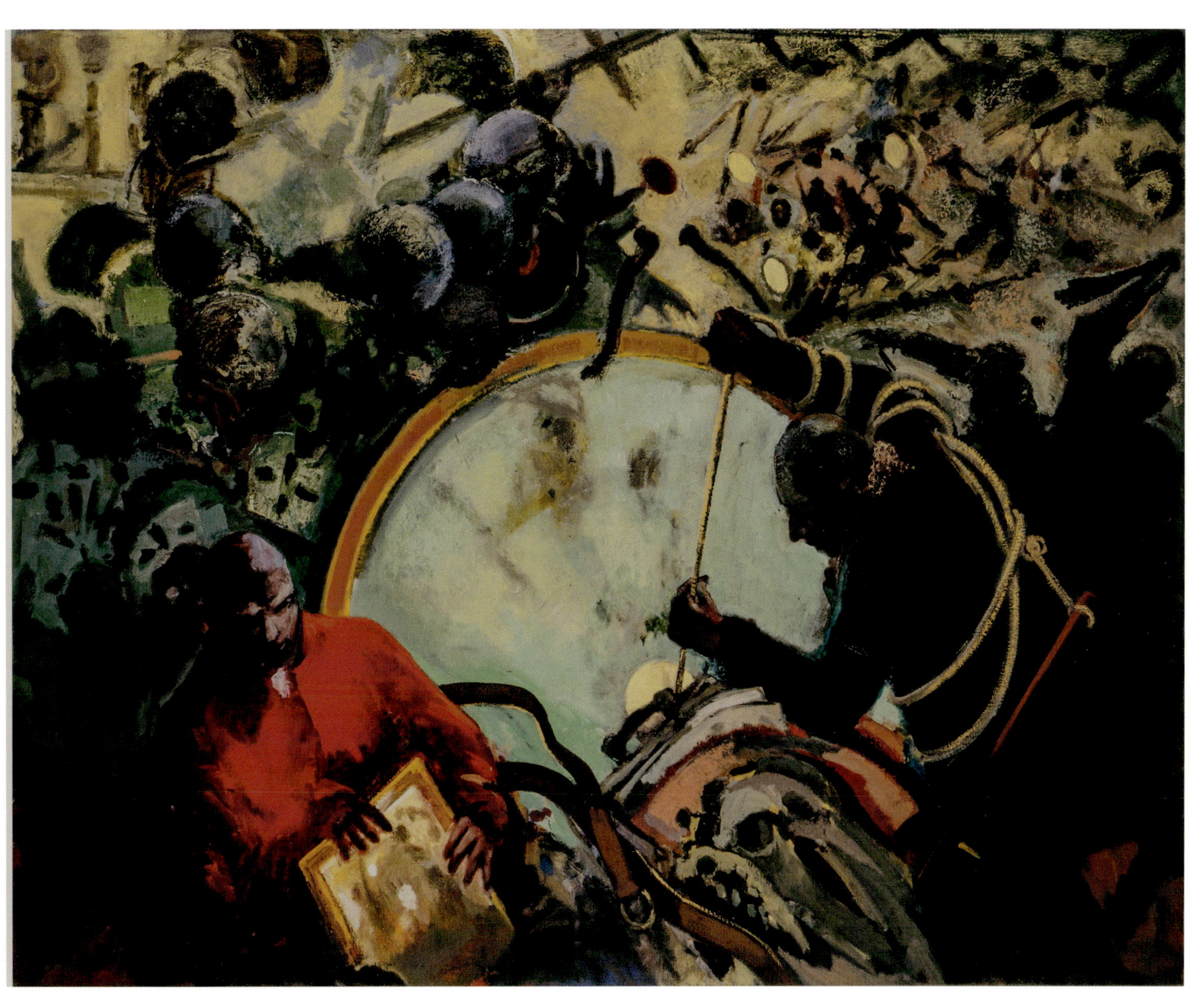

PLATE 11

Ursula, 1996
Series: Blood and Perfume
Oil on canvas
61 x 62 (155 x 157.5)
Collection of Ani Afsar

According to Jacques Collin de Plancy's 1821 *Critical Dictionary of Relics and Miraculous Images*, Saint Ursula went to sea to meet her betrothed with 11,000 handmaidens, represented here by the walking figures along the periphery of the picture plane. After the boat makes a miraculous journey in a single day, Ursula decides to make a pilgrimage to Rome instead of marrying, and she and her entourage eventually go to Cologne, where all are killed by the Huns. The haloed saint rests in her blood-red sarcophagus, draped in a garland of fragrant flowers. The artist—seen in a framed portrait at the bottom—records the events.

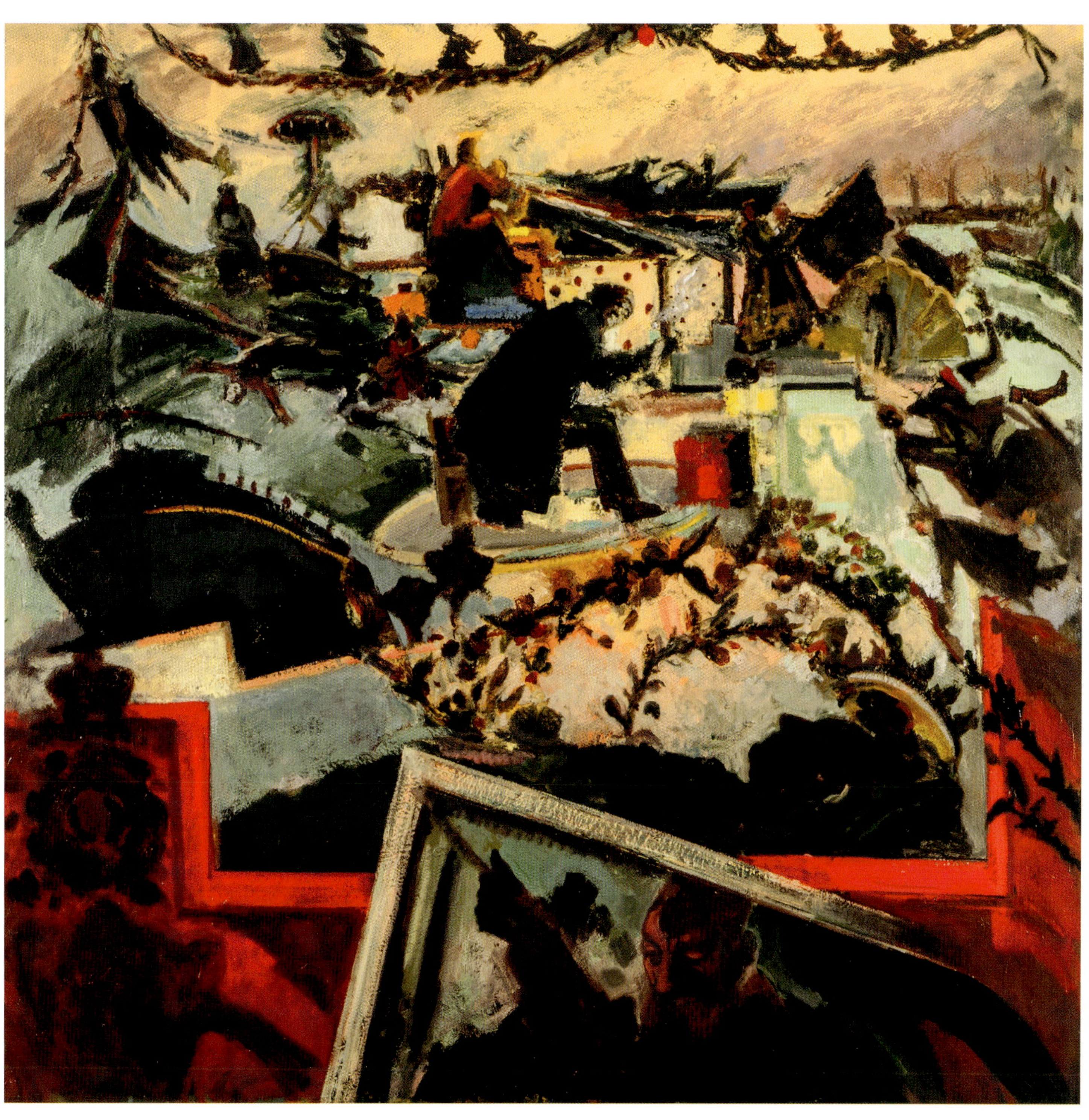

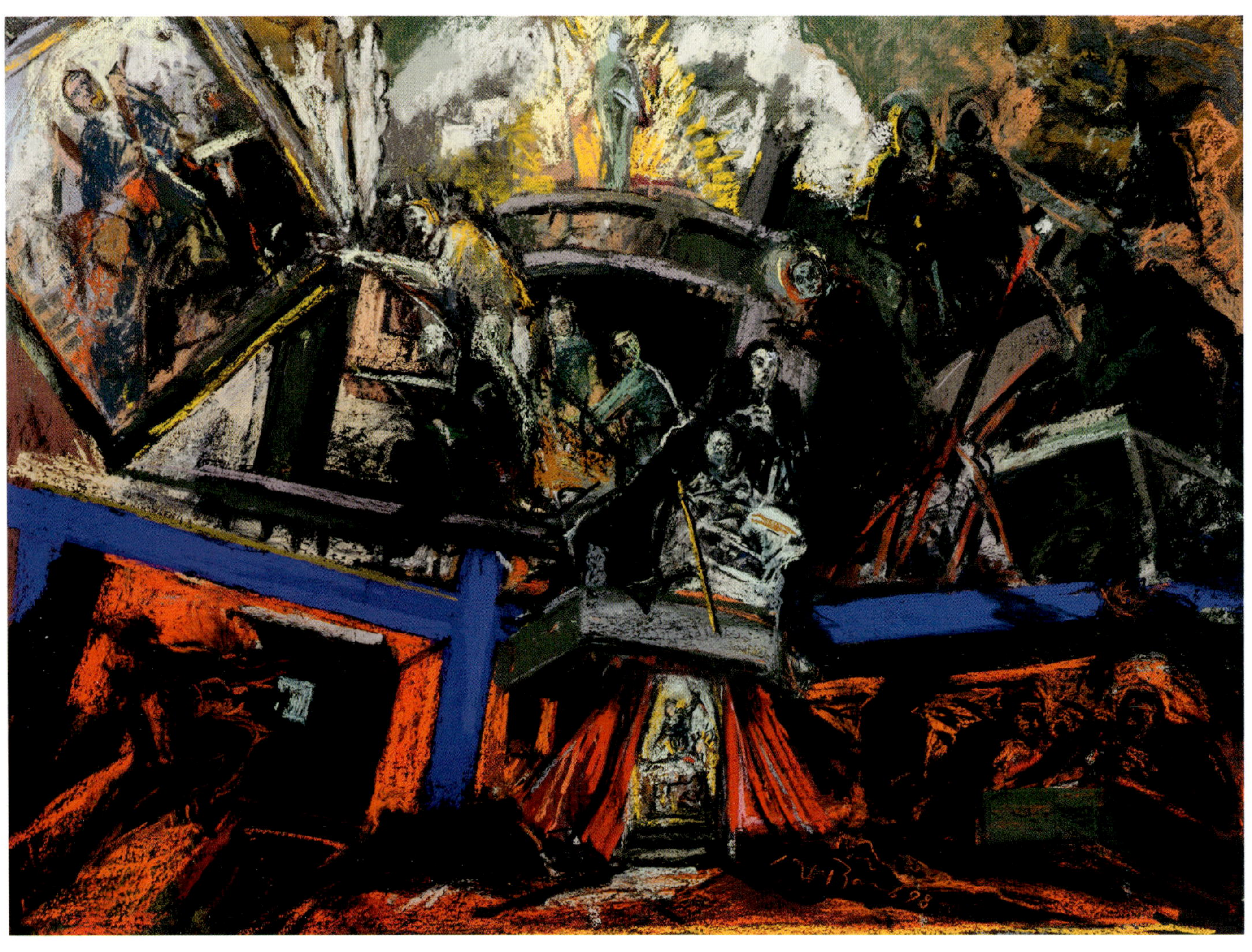

PLATE 12

Macbeth, 1998
Pastel on paper
21 7/16 x 29 1/2 (54.5 x 74.9)
Collection of Laura and Larry Gerber

Among Barnes's most overtly theatrical compositions, this drawing is a pastiche of scenes from William Shakespeare's Scottish tragedy *Macbeth*. The character of Banquo is seen in the top center with his family below him on the stage, while in the lower center between parted red curtains, Macbeth is glimpsed stabbing King Duncan, spurred on by the prophecy of the Three Witches. The aftermath of his action is alluded to by the ghostly and skeletal figures, off-kilter lines, and palette of electric blue and orange. The ancestral portrait (Barnes in a kilt) in the upper left corner alludes to the fact that the artist is a descendent of the Macbeth clan and, thus, in some sense, heir to its tragic legacy.

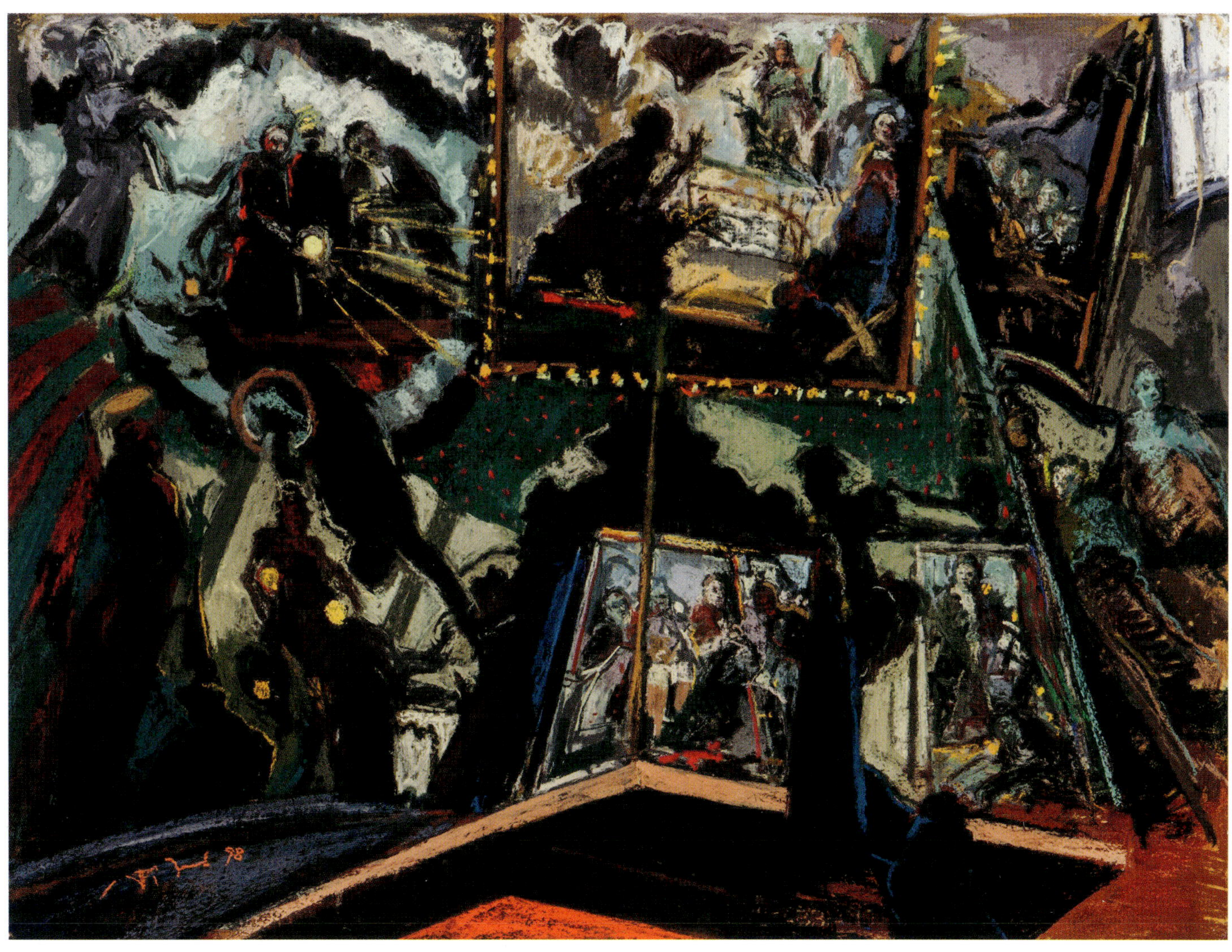

PLATE 13

Cinema alla Rocca, 1998
Pastel on paper
30 ¼ x 37 ½ (76.8 x 95.3)
Collection of Paul Caccia and Carmela Zammuto

In an ironic juxtaposition of past and present, Barnes recalls a summer tradition in a small Umbrian town near his Italian home, where contemporary movies are shown on the exterior wall of a twelfth-century prison. Seemingly oblivious to the horrors and suffering witnessed by those walls—as represented the ghostly figures on the right-hand side—the audience gathers below a screen ringed with marque lights; the projectionists can be seen in the upper left.

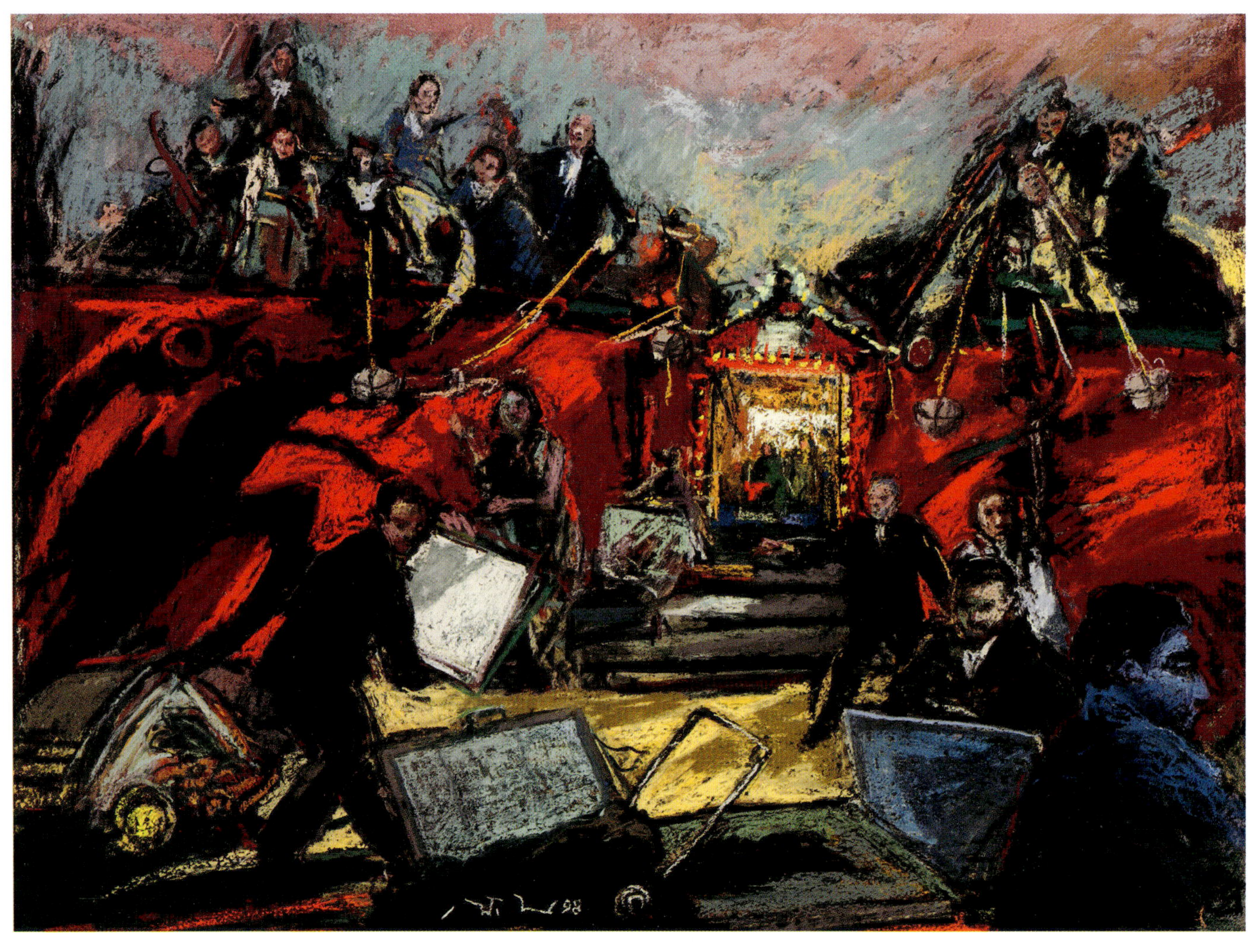

PLATE 14

The Young Artist Approaching the Temple of Art, 1998
Pastel on paper
21 ½ x 29 ½ (54.6 x 74.9)
Collection of Laura and Larry Gerber

Throughout Barnes's oeuvre, references to the creative process can be found, such as a small fire signifying a spark of inspiration, plumb bobs, or the jutting corners of a picture frame. However, this image offers a more direct commentary on the business of art. In the foreground, young artists, including Barnes's daughter and future son-in-law (shown twice), arrive with portfolios in hand at an art gallery. Seen as a "temple of art" with a central altar surrounded by gold coins, the inner sanctum includes a celestial realm filled with figures dangling bait, such as fame and fortune. Just in front of the temple is a money changer at a table, while to the right Barnes tries to caution the naïve youngsters. The black shape in the foreground suggests a large mousetrap.

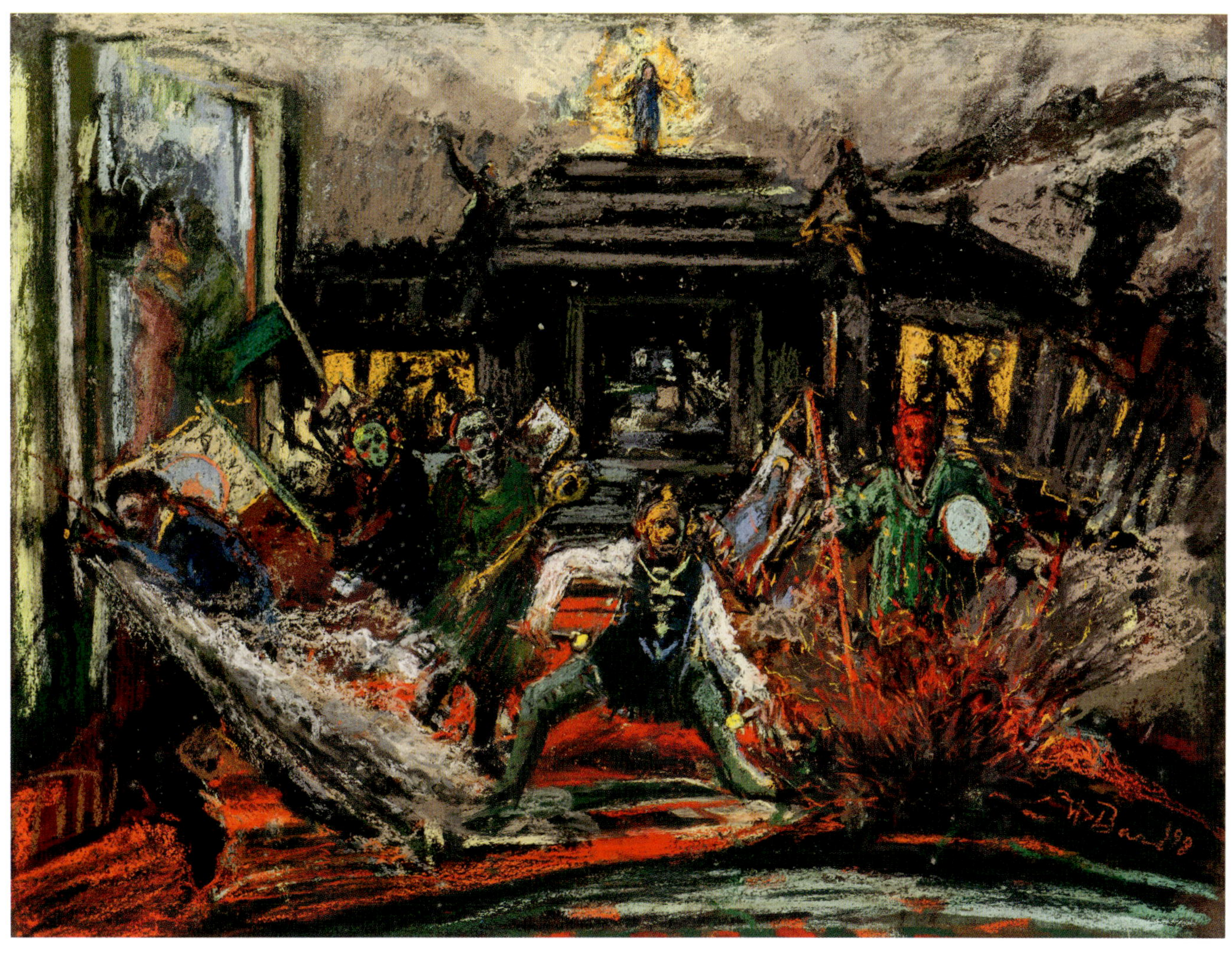

PLATE 15

The Dance of the Tre Potencias, 1998
Pastel on paper
22 ⅛ x 29 ⅞ (56.2 x 75.9)
Collection of Linda Kramer and Mary Kennedy

Barnes took his inspiration for this image from a folk dance he saw performed on a visit to New Mexico. The dance features two figures representing evil (suggested by the devilish character on the right) and good (as seen on the left, under a hastily copulating couple). As the battle/dance progresses, a third figure appears as a shamanic entity that comes between them. First "good" is chased away and then "evil" burns up in an explosion of fireworks. Only the enigmatic final dancer remains, resulting in a draw. Although the dance evokes a pagan ritual, the figure of the Virgin Mary tops the temple edifice in the background.

PLATE 16

Hawthorn, 2000
Series: The Ogham
Oil on canvas
65 ⅛ x 60 ¼ (165.4 x 153)
Collection of Laura and Larry Gerber

In the ancient Celtic alphabet known as the Ogham, letters are associated with certain trees, animals, and symbolic meanings. *Huath*, represented by the sturdy little hawthorn tree, equates to contradictions, consequences, and relationships. The hawthorn tree is itself a study in duality: full of beautiful blossoms in the spring, but covered with sharp thorns; a source of powerful medicine, but bad luck to bring into the house (its cut branches smell like decomposing flesh); imbued with male energy, but associated with the female goddess. In this image, a fox seeks refuge in a hawthorn thicket, thwarting a trio of hunters who approach from the right. The curvilinear, balanced composition suggests that neither predator nor prey has the upper hand.

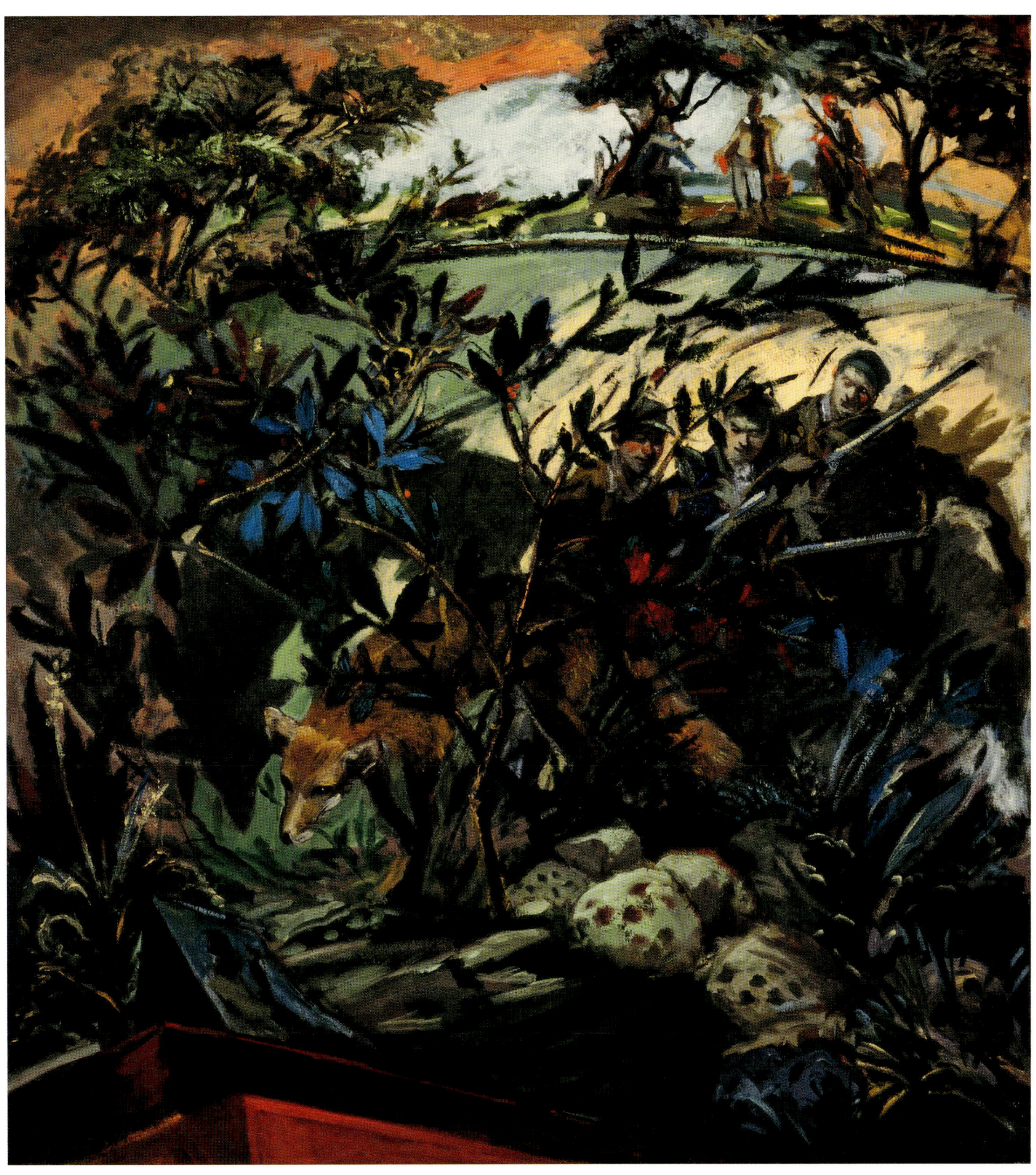

PLATE 17

Mistletoe, 2000
Series: The Ogham
Oil on canvas
66 ¾ x 61 ½ (169.5 x 156.2)
Collection of Paul Caccia and Carmela Zammuto

Though no letter in the Ogham alphabet is associated with mistletoe, it was considered the most mystical and magical of all of the plants revered by the Druids, because as a semi-parasite it could live on many other trees, including the mighty oak. As an evergreen it also stood out in the winter months, when all else was bare. Mistletoe was thought to heal illness and foster good health, provide protection, afford successful hunting, exorcise demons, and bestow fertility. In this image, mistletoe hangs above a vase of flowers in a windowsill. The female figure on the right-hand side is fleeing from its powers, while a Barnes avatar—a fox which he associates with passion—looks on.

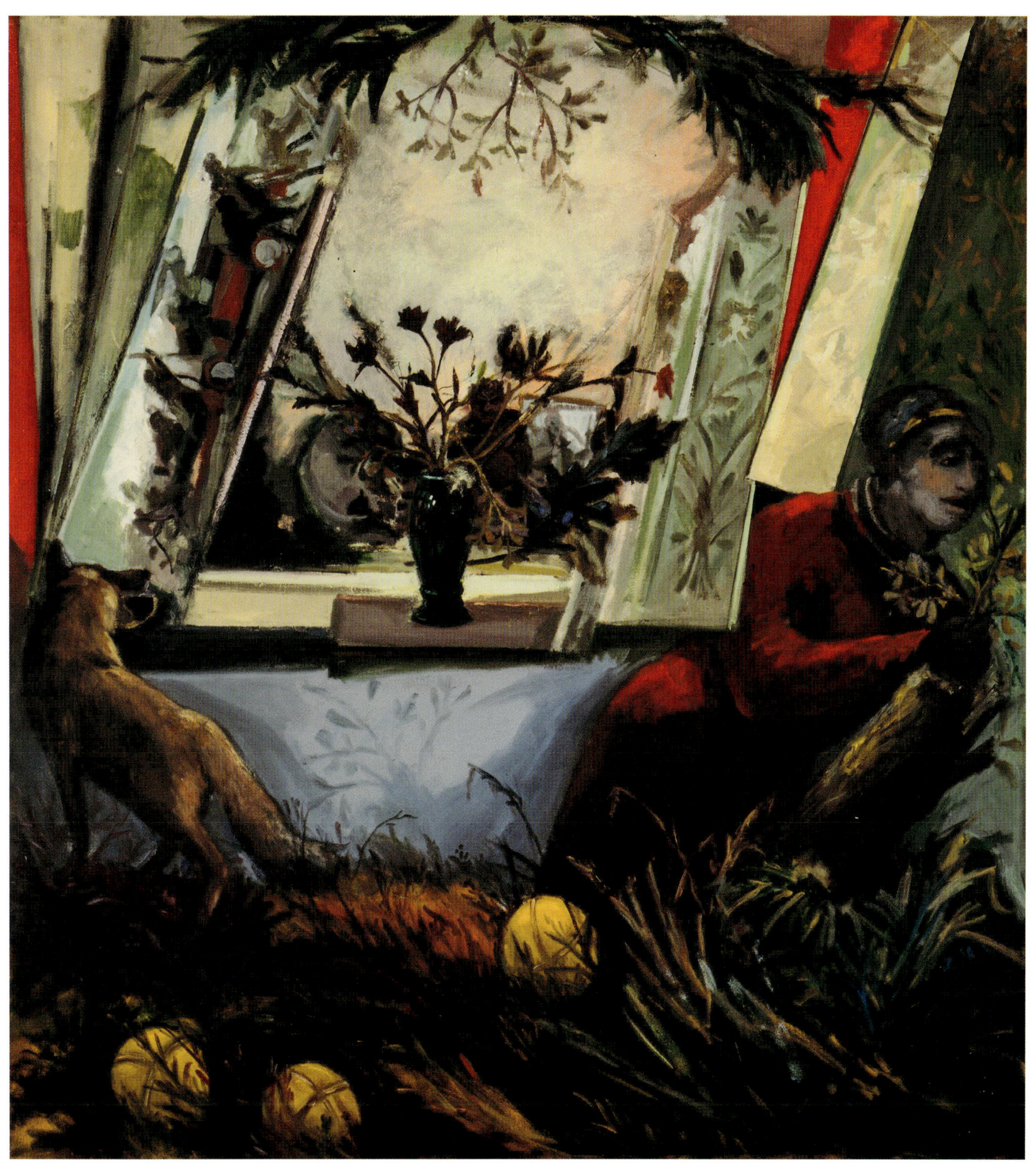

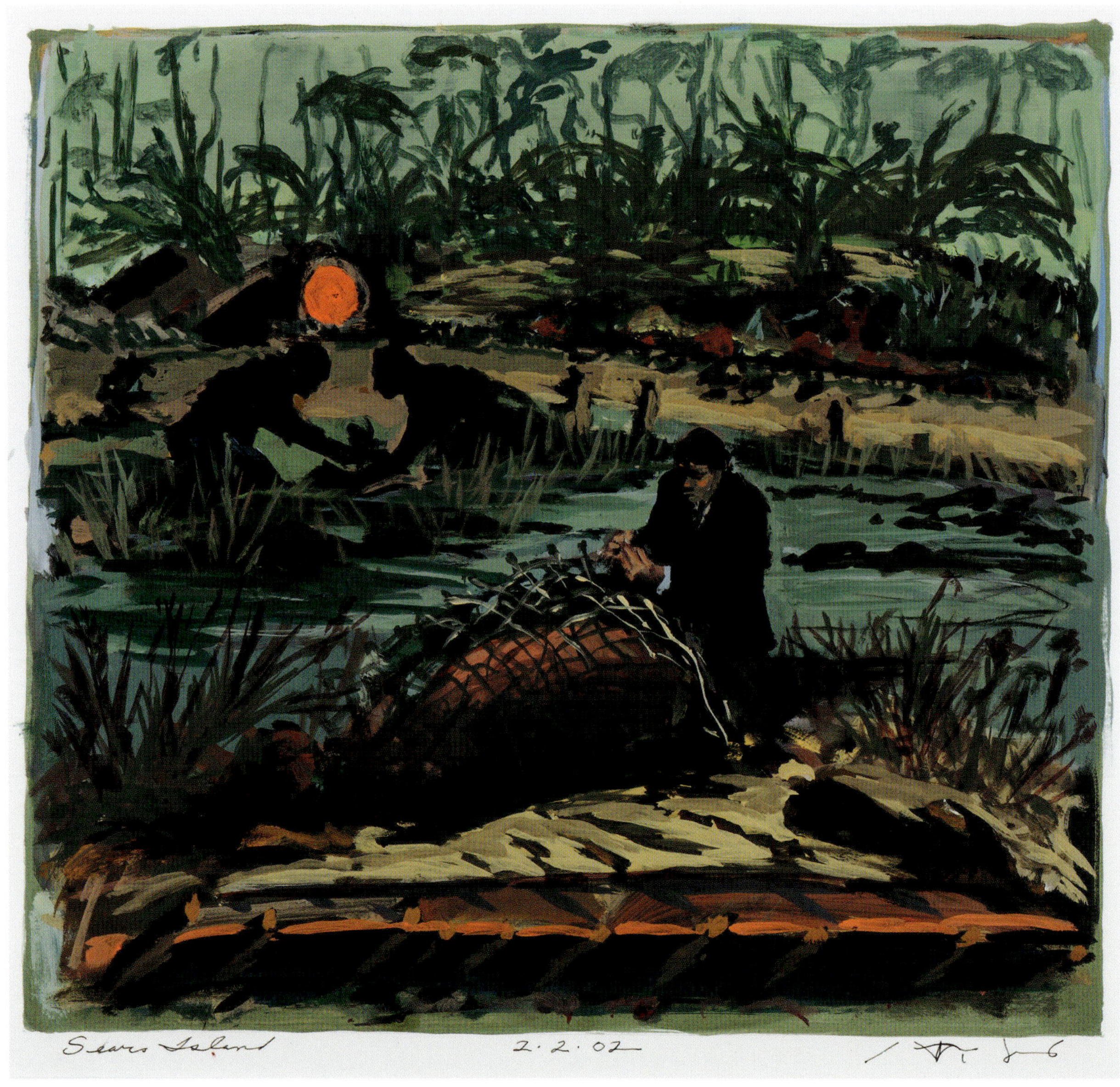

PLATE 18

Sears Island, 2002
Series: The Penobscot
Casein on paper
22 ⅛ x 29 ¾ (56.2 x 75.6)
Collection of Lawrence and Evelyn Aronson

This scene takes place on Sears Island near Barnes's home in Searsport, Maine. The state-owned land is the largest undeveloped, uninhabited, causeway-accessible island on the eastern coast of the United States. Going back to the time of the indigenous Wabanaki confederation, it has served hunters and gatherers digging during low tide for shellfish, seaweed, or other natural bounty. The figure in the foreground is mending a net, while the pair of shadowy figures silhouetted by a bright orange beacon adds a sense of danger and mystery to the action.

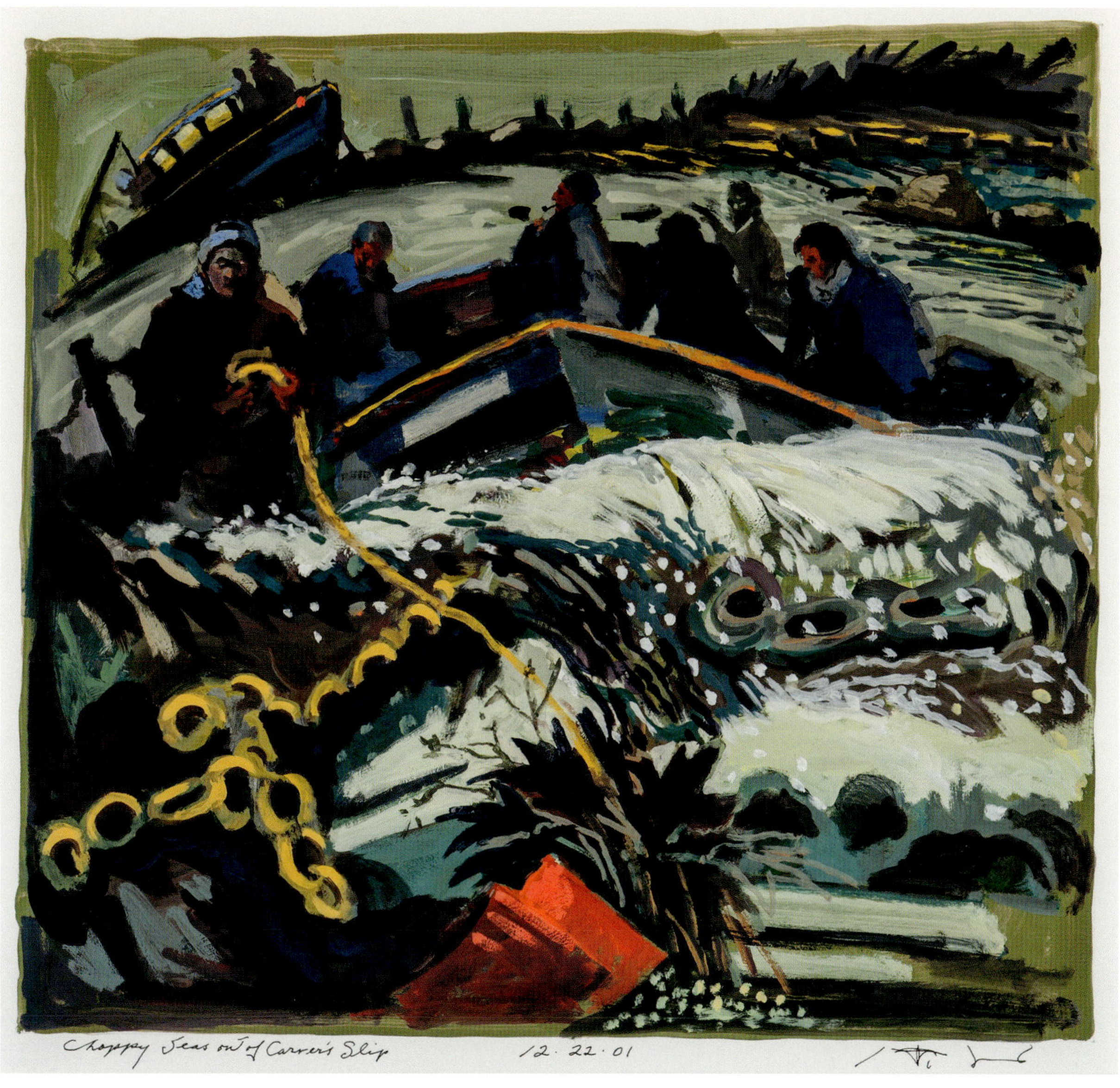

PLATE 19

Choppy Seas Out of Carver's Slip, 2001
Series: The Penobscot
Casein on paper
22 x 30 (55.9 x 76.2)
Collection of Lisa and Tim Wittman, Chicago

Carver's Slip is just across the street from Barnes's home, the historic Carver House built around 1816 by a local shipbuilder. This image shows the rugged seas that are characteristic of the Maine coast. Although the central boat appears to be tethered to the shore as evinced by the rope and chains in the lower left corner, the waves remain foreboding. The small still-life in the foreground recalls the flotsam that regularly accumulates on the beach. The lights of the boat in the background and the blue-tinged palette suggest a cold dawn or dusk: as they have for centuries, Maine fishermen go out to sea in the early morning and return in the dark during the short daylight hours of the winter months.

PLATE 20

The Mackerel Run—Belfast Harbor, 2002
Series: The Penobscot
Casein on paper
22 5⁄16 x 30 (56.7 x 76.2)
Collection of the Indiana University Art Museum; Museum purchase with funds from the Elizabeth P. Myers Art Acquisition Endowment Fund, 2002.27

Recalling the Japonisme aesthetic of Vincent van Gogh, Barnes transforms a beloved fishing tradition of summer in southern Maine into a festival of sparkling lights: reflected off the waves, in the stars in the sky, from the lanterns on the bridge that are mirrored in the dark water, and through the windows of the passing boat. The image also recalls the cycle of life—when the mackerel come in, they are devoured by seals which, in turn, are eaten by sharks.

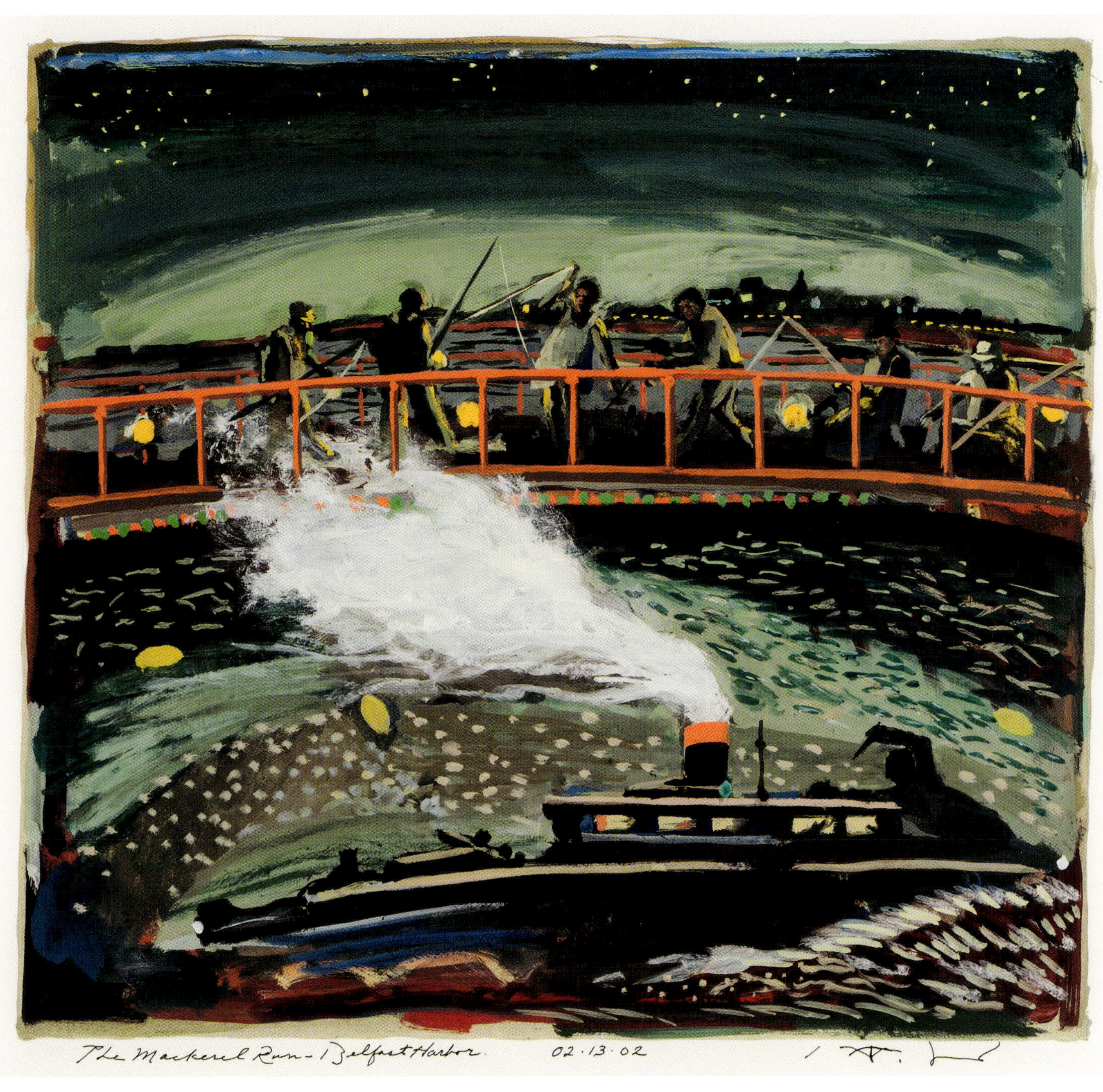
The Mackerel Run - Belfast Harbor.
02·13·02

PLATE 21

Self-Portrait Vanitas, 2002
Series: Vanitas
Oil on panel
24 ½ x 47 13⁄16 (62.2 x 121.4)
Collection of Willie Kohler and Shauna Angel Blue

Created when the artist was age sixty-eight, this vanitas suggests the passing of time and the futility of ego. Although the artist is seen in one of his few recognizable portraits, the brush is in the hand of Death rather than his own. It is the skull that wears the victor's laurels. Canvases with their backs toward the viewer fill the composition, while the shadowy dancing figures that populate so many of Barnes's images frolic as a border decoration on the wall. Barnes's favorite plant, mistletoe, which he associates with power, is seen in the upper left, while a clump of seaweed rests on the frame in the foreground. In the background, a mirror reflects the artist in his studio, indicating that he is still in control of the illusion.

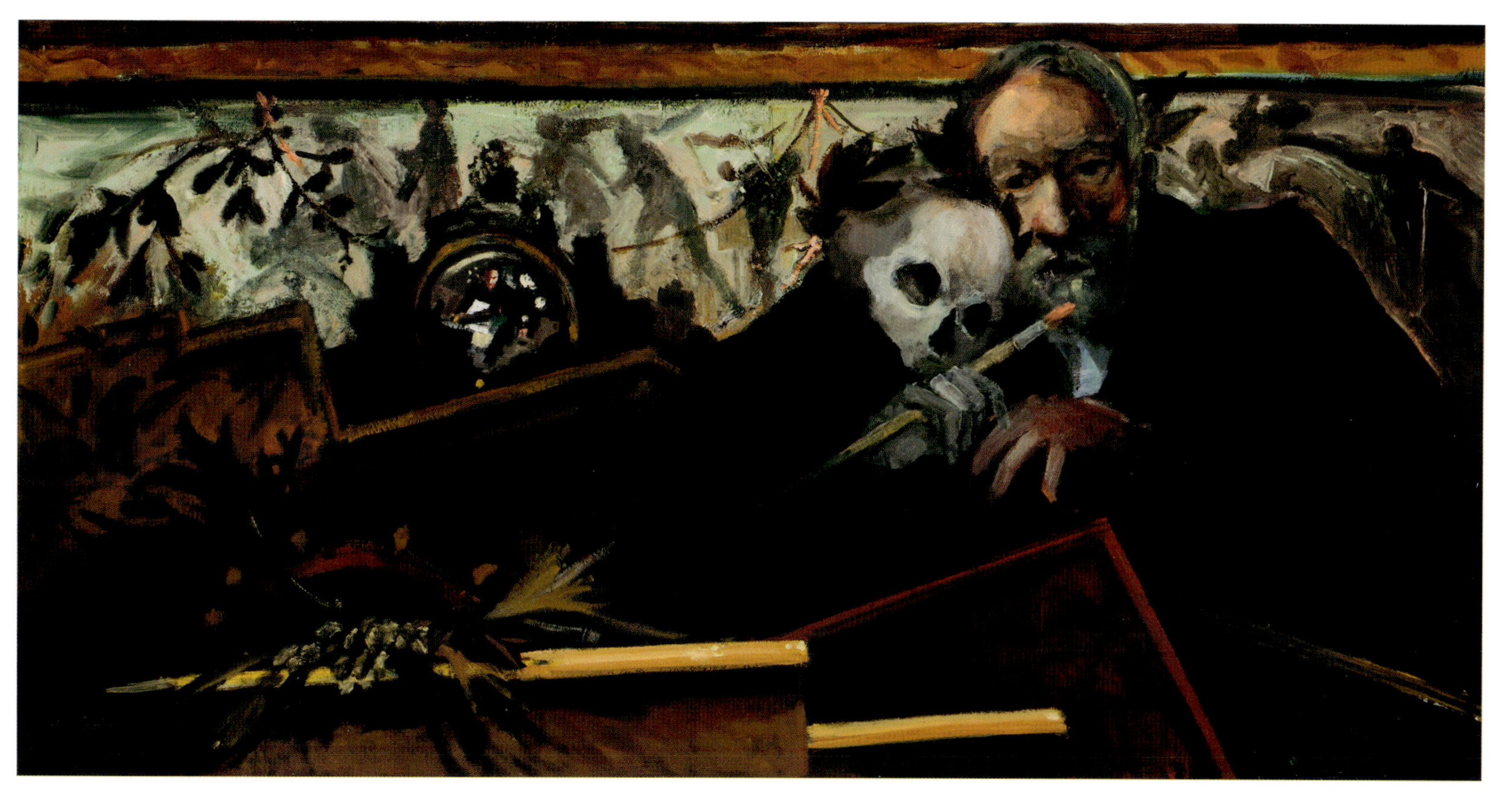

PLATE 22

Death Curse, 2004
Series: Jettatura
Oil on canvas
69 x 64 (175.3 x 163.6)
Collection of Aileen and John Schloerb
Photo: Tim Johnson

Iettatura (Jettatura in its anglicized spelling) is an archaic Italian word meaning "to throw," referring to the casting of the evil eye. Anyone whom the "cursed" looks upon will suffer bad luck. Unfortunately, the agent of misfortune doesn't always intend that outcome. There is inherent tragedy in someone who becomes the unwitting bearer of ill-fortune and as a result becomes a social pariah (note the whispering figures in the background). The cross-shaped pack of cards wrapped in a black crepe ribbon holds death curses between each sheet. It is unclear whether the man passing the message to the seated figure knows the evil lurking within. This image was based on Barnes's visit to the museum of anthropology in Perugia, which has an extensive collection of amulets and talismans.

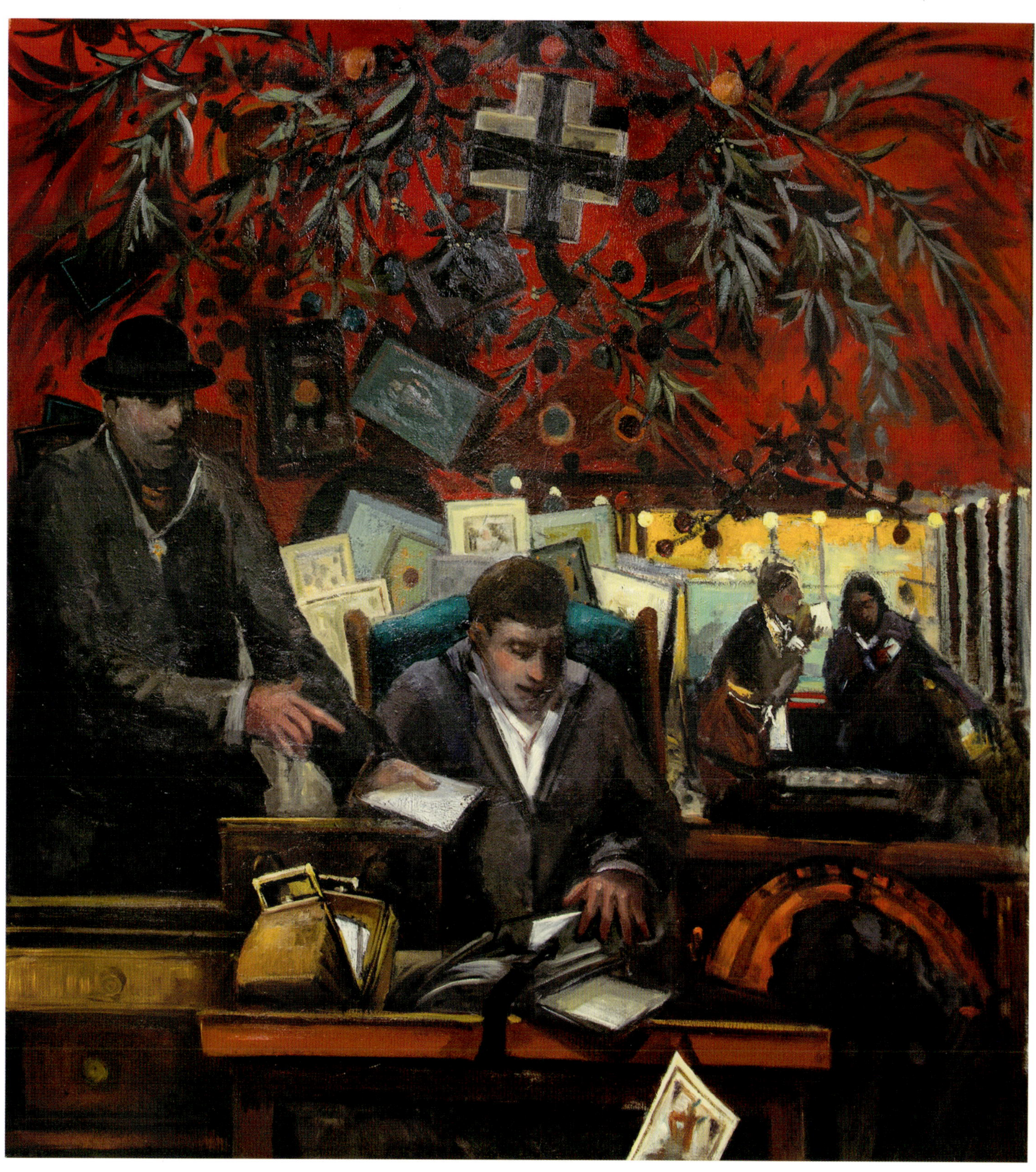

PLATE 23

Pietra e Fulmine, 2004
Series: Jettatura
Oil on canvas
69 ⅛ x 64 ⅛ (165.4 x 153)
Collection of Paul Caccia and Carmela Zammuto

Based on the artist's travels and family life, this image holds a deep personal connection. The phrase *pietra e fulmine*, stone and lightning, refers to an old Italian folk remedy of using a magical stone that has been hit by lightning to treat epilepsy, a condition afflicting the artist's daughter and all of her children. Some of these stones are enshrined with ribbons on the upper left, while storm clouds gather on the upper right. The workman walking through the garden suggests a local bringing a token of well wishes. The haloed artist observes the actions from a yellow enclosure in the center of the composition, while his wife Nancy appears behind him. Barnes recalls that the Umbrians, who adhered to many old superstitions, considered his daughter to be magical.

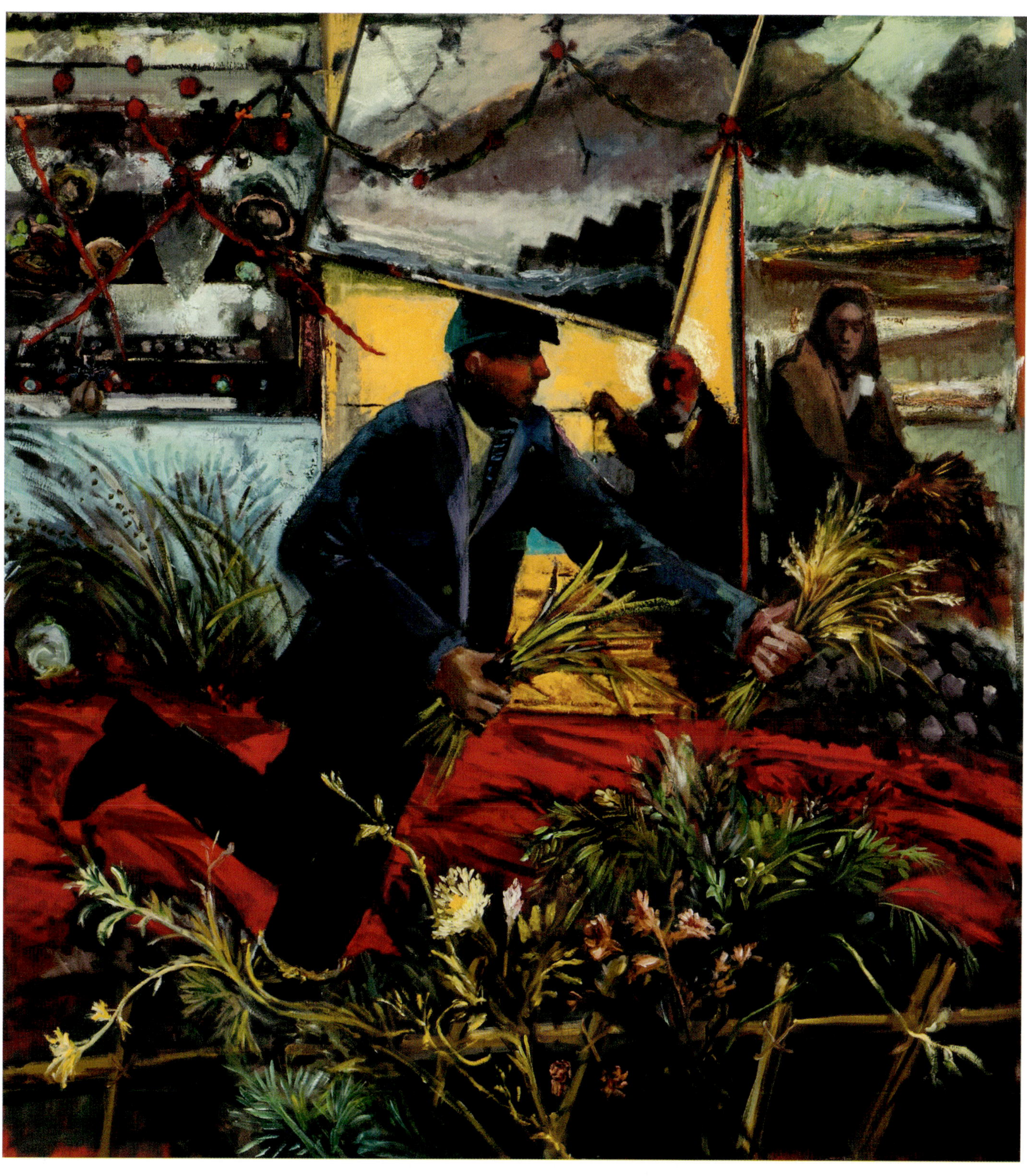

PLATE 24

I Brevi, 2004
Series: Jettatura
Oil on canvas
69 x 64 (175.3 x 162.9)
Collection of Laura and Larry Gerber
Photo: Tim Johnson

Inspired by a vast collection of amulets in the Museo Archeologico Nazionale dell' Umbria, this image reflects their continued use in the rural communities of central and southern Italy. Reflecting an interesting mixture of Catholicism and pre-Christian paganism, these magical objects were used to bring good luck, ward off the evil eye, and protect a person's health, animals, and property. Some amulets contained *brevi*, written prayers or spells. These sayings were sealed in a packet and worn around the owner's neck. The composition shows the process of creating an amulet, from raw materials to purchase. A string of amulets hangs across the top, while a shadowy scene on the upper right suggests a threatening catastrophe.

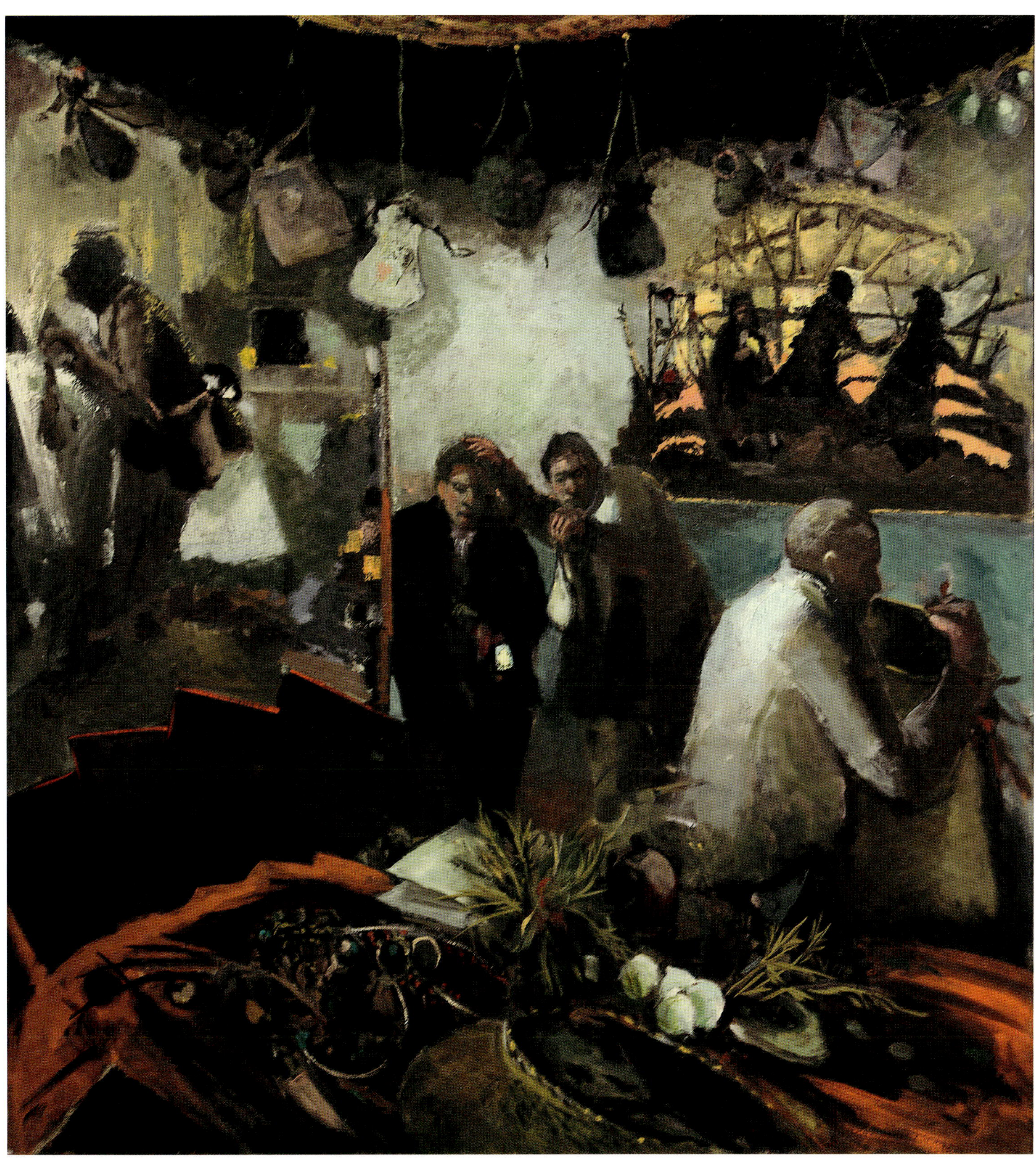

PLATE 25

The Laureate, 2006
Pastel on paper
22 ½ x 26 (57.2 x 66)
Collection of Lisa and Tim Wittman, Chicago

This picture pays homage to the nineteenth-century French symbolist Paul Verlaine, one of Barnes's favorite poets. Verlaine's behavior was considered scandalous, and his works were criticized by traditionalists because of their unconventional style and sexual themes. However, here "the Master" or the "Prince of Poets" (as he was known to his followers) is being lauded for his achievements by a muse holding a laurel wreath above his head. The seated figure on the left-hand side represents another poet or young literary admirer. Accolades, however, can often prove to be a burden. The shadows on the wall suggest the ideas in Verlaine's poetry, to which he is struggling to return.

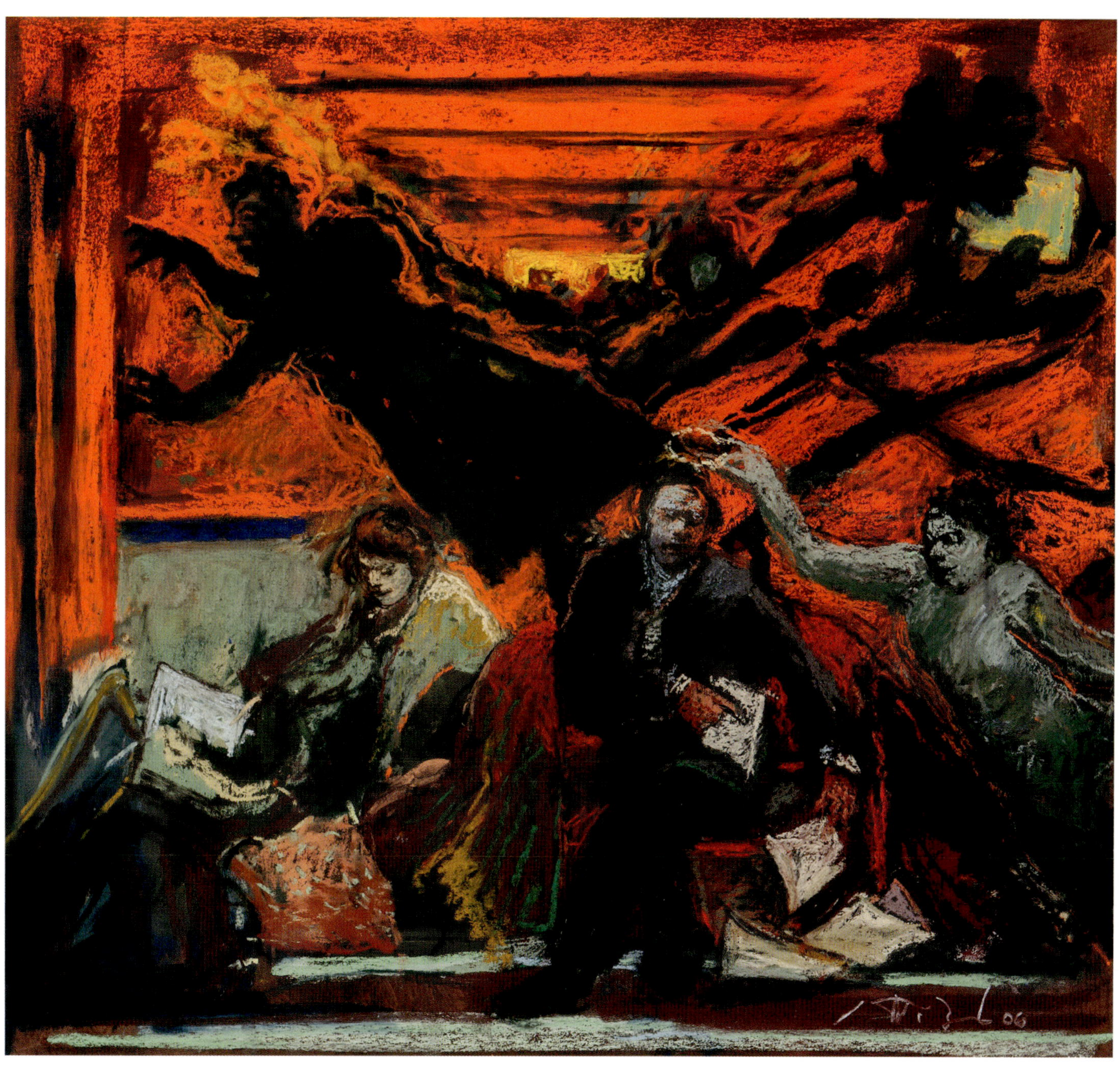

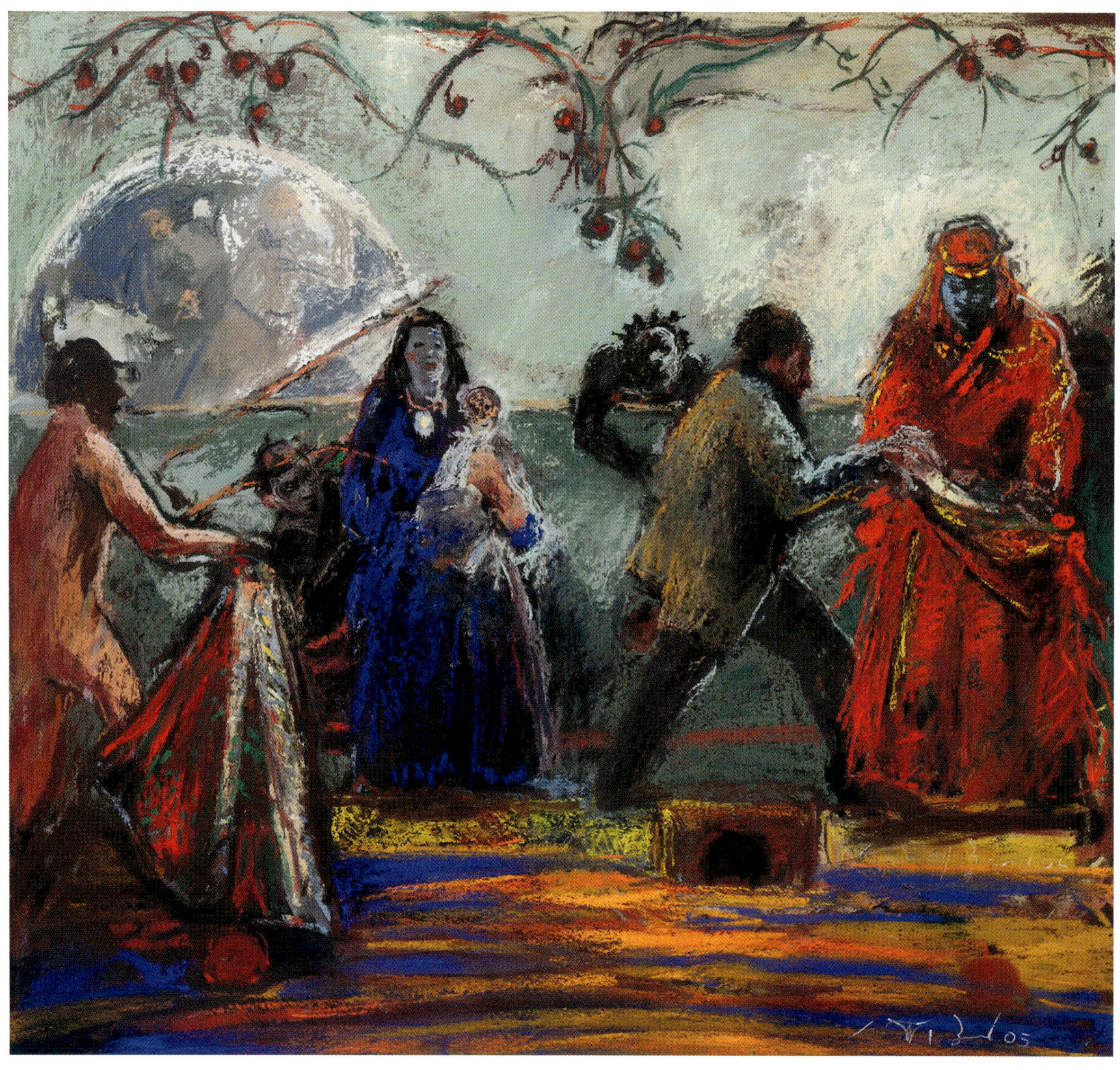

PLATE 26

The Most Beautiful Man in the World, 2005
Pastel on paper
22 5⁄8 x 26 1⁄8 (57.5 x 66.2)
Collection of John Jones

During his early years in New York City, Barnes intersected with a notable group of artists, including Marcel Duchamp, Alexander Calder, and Roberto Matta. One of these memorable figures was the artist Paul Swan. Barnes recalls not only the wonderful "recitals" in his studio at Carnegie Hall, but also his host's eccentricities, including his vanity and his penchant for dressing up in togas (which were easier to remove when showing his "perfect" skin). In this image, Swan appears twice, draped and undraped. The Madonna-like figure presiding with him symbolizes Swan's wife holding their child.

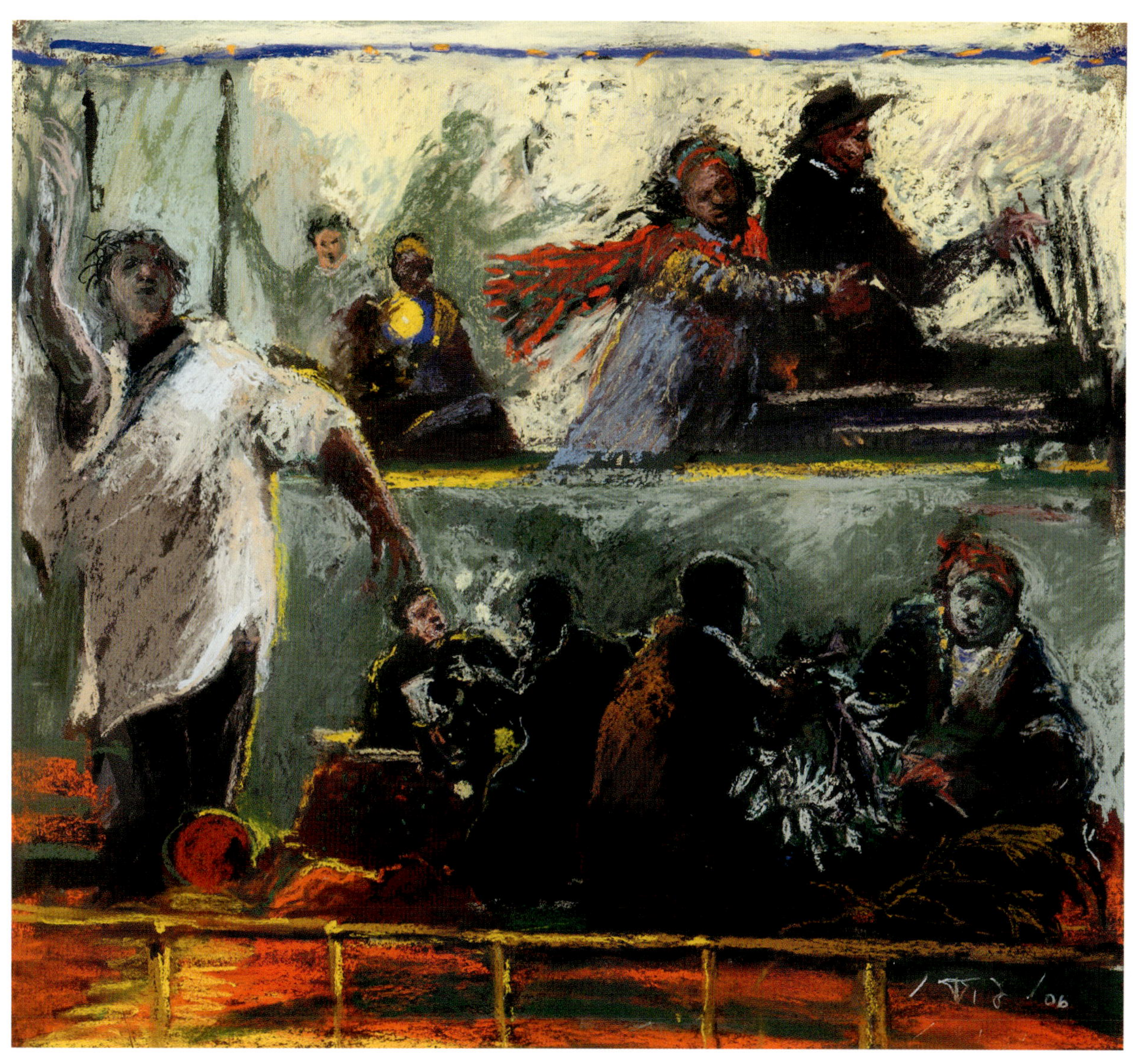

PLATE 27

Swan's Eulogy for Isadora Duncan, 2006
Pastel on paper
22 5/8 x 26 1/16 (57.5 x 66.8)
Collection of Laura and Larry Gerber

The upper and lower registers of this picture depict events from two different time periods. The top section refers to the final car ride of the great modern-dance pioneer Isadora Duncan, who was killed when the long silk scarf she was wearing became entangled in the wheels of her convertible. The lower half of the composition imagines the eulogy presented by the artist Paul Swan at her funeral. Although Swan gestures dramatically while wearing a toga (a favored costume of both Swan and Duncan), the seated figures busy making a memorial wreath seem largely disinterested in his theatrics.

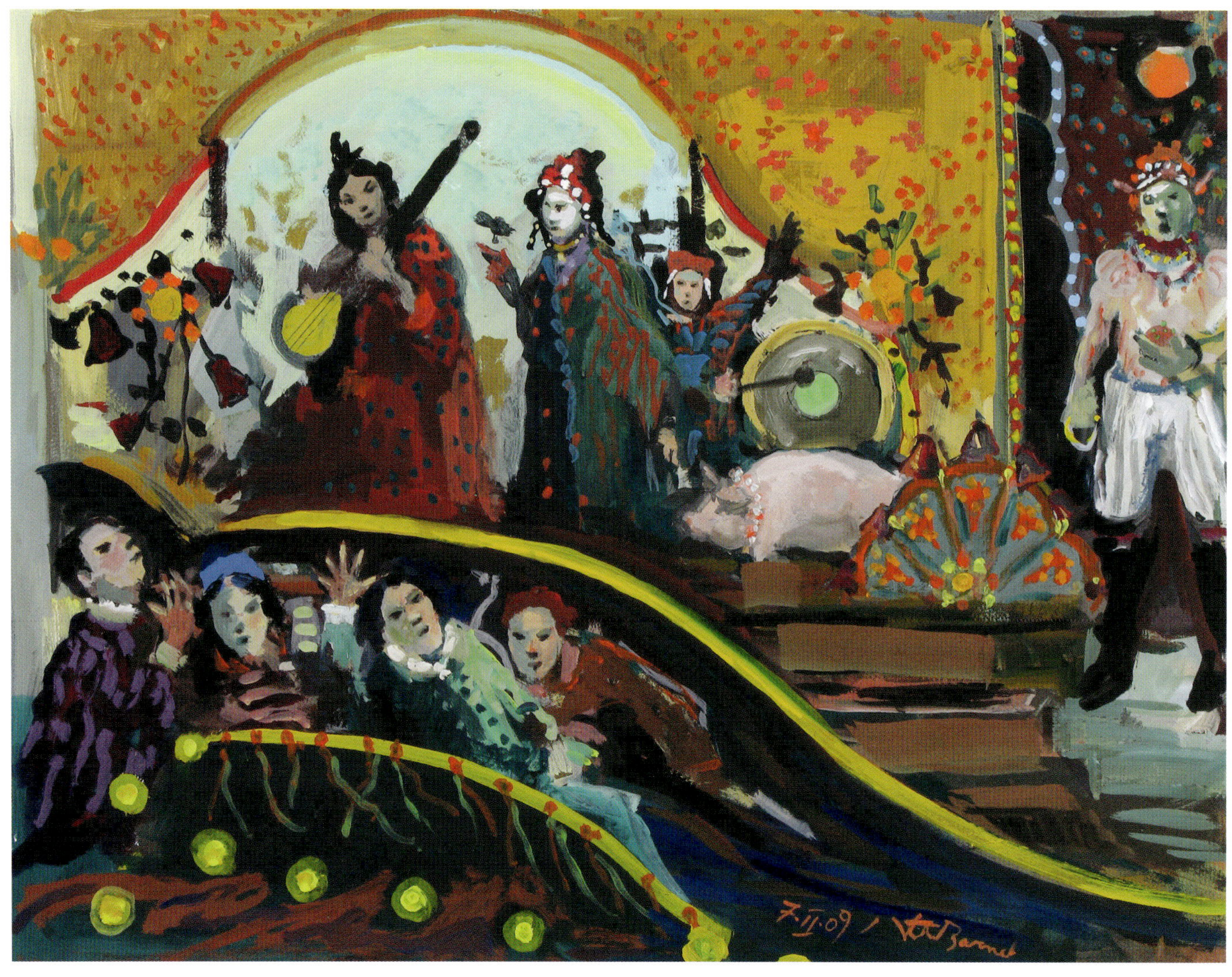

PLATE 28

Chinese Opera, 2009
Casein on paper
23 x 30 (58.4 x 76.2)
Collection of Paul Caccia and Carmela Zammuto

In his early years in New York City, Barnes lived on Delancey Street between Little Italy and Chinatown, an eclectic neighborhood that exposed him to new cultural experiences that he would recall throughout his life. This image, replete with the vibrant colors and patterns that caught his attention both on the stage and in the audience, recalls the many theatrical performances that he saw in a small Chinese theater. Since he didn't understand the language, he relied on the repetition of many stock characters and props, including the frequent appearance of a pig.

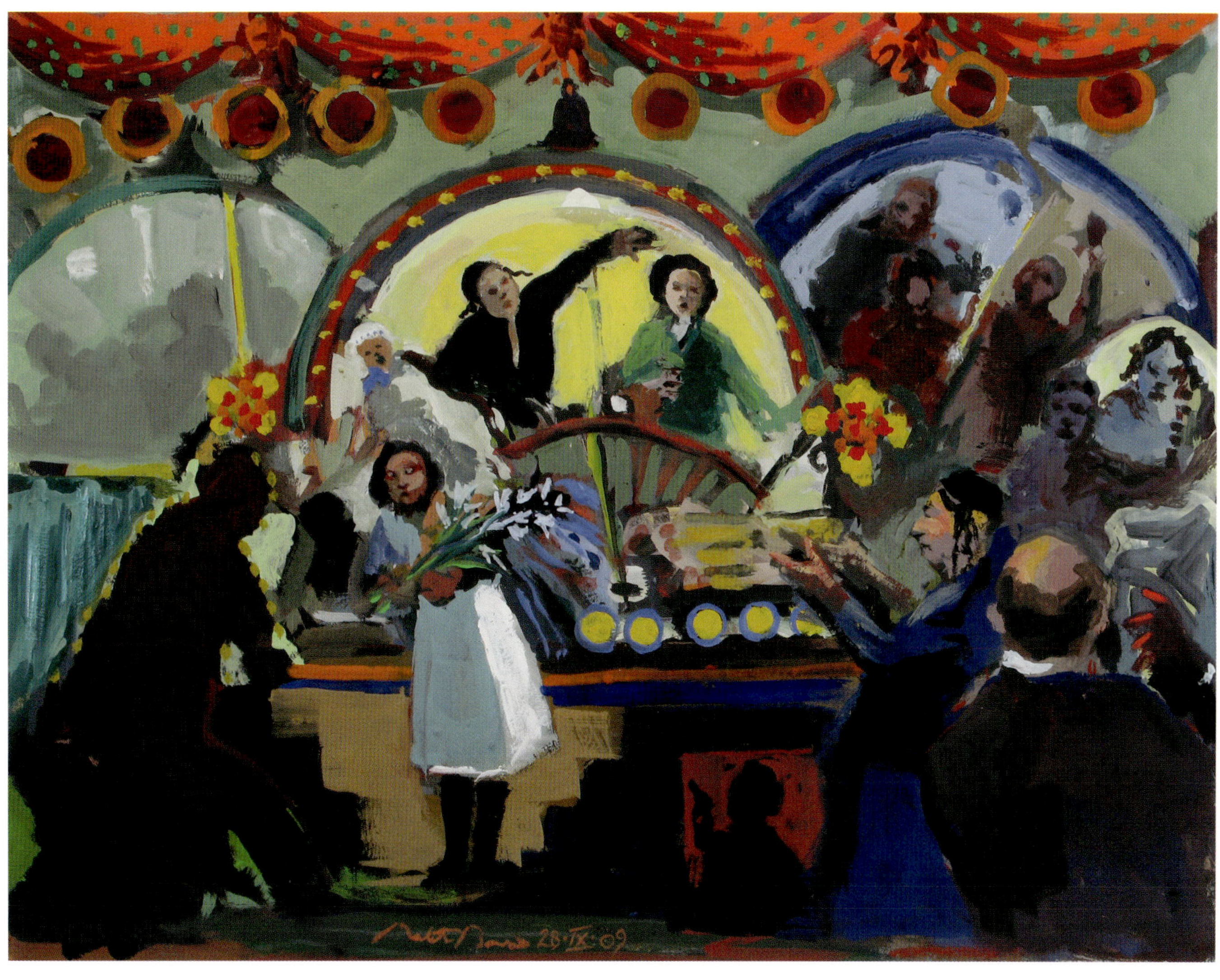

PLATE 29

The Yiddish Theatre on Hester Street, 2009
Casein on paper
23 x 30 (58.4 x 76.2)
Collection of Laura and Larry Gerber

Recalling Barnes's memories of living in New York City near the Lower East Side, this image plays on the stock characters featured in Yiddish theater, such as the henpecked husband (Shmendrik) and his irritating wife, seen near the center of the composition. Barnes enjoyed the sound of the Yiddish language and the sense of humor conveyed by these productions. He had always been drawn to the theater and even considered becoming an actor before turning to the visual arts. Barnes recalled that it was the artist Marcel Duchamp who suggested that he treat "painting as a stage." As such, his images often feature a shallow depth of field, a proscenium-like framing, and an array of characters in concurrent scenes.

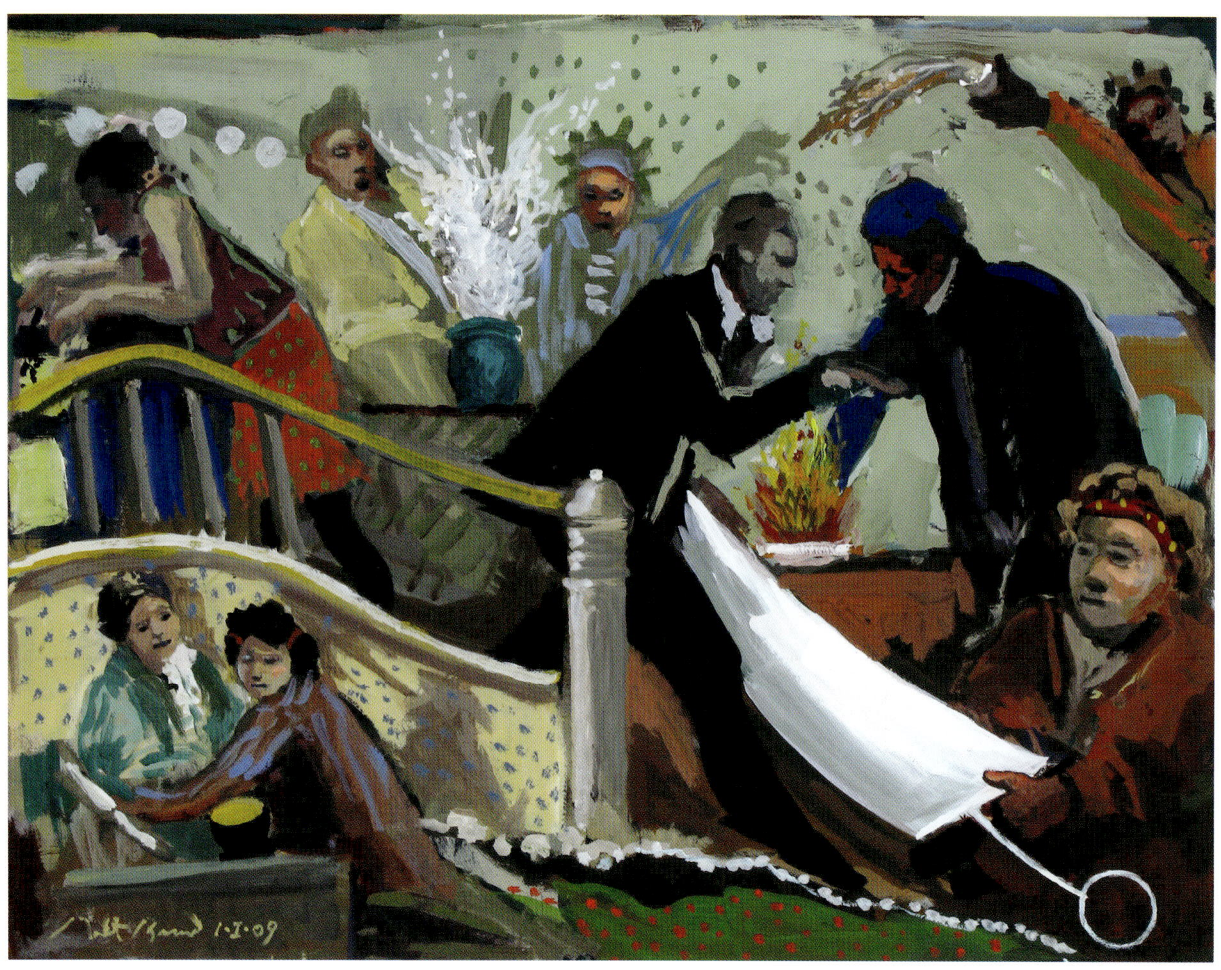

PLATE 30

The House of Secrets, 2009
Casein on paper
23 x 30 (58.4 x 76.2)
Collection of Laura and Larry Gerber

The social sin of gossiping is identified with an evil tongue, while its practitioners are known as backbiters. This series of vignettes depicts couples apparently sharing secrets, perhaps about the young woman on the balcony. The exploding jar represents the bad karma that can come back to punish the gossipers as a result of their malicious rumors. The older woman in the lower right holding a roller shade refers to one of the artist's earliest memories, while also suggesting a kind of artistic voyeurism.

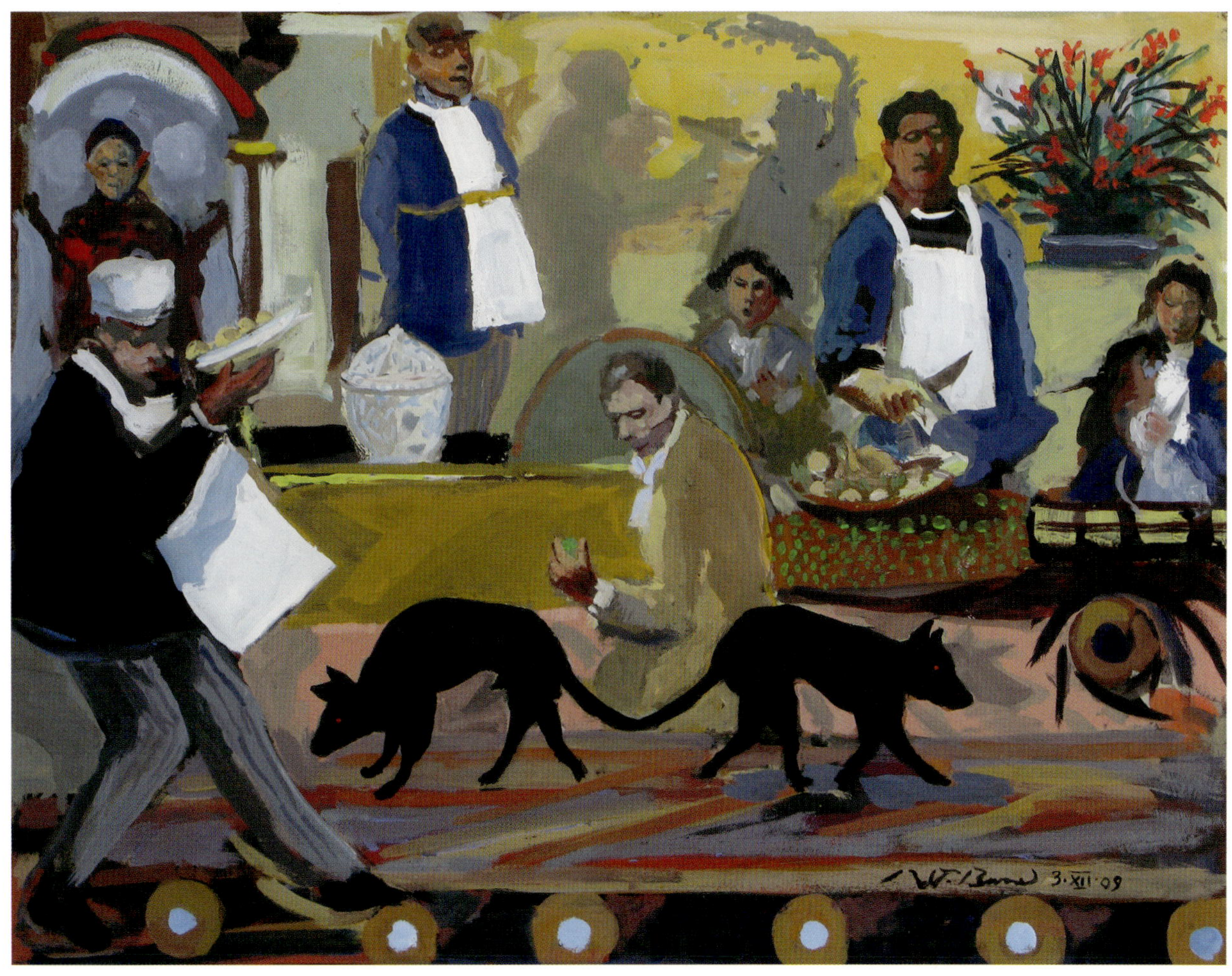

PLATE 31

Two Dogs, 2009
Casein on paper
23 x 30 (58.4 x 76.2)
Collection of Rolf Achilles and Maral Hashemi

Two of Barnes's favorite themes throughout his career are waiters (often falling) and dogs. These dogs often connote a more serious meaning than is immediately apparent. In Barnes's personal iconography, the black dog represents death that is tracking you down. In this case the tails of the dogs are tied together; thus, as the man with the glass at the center of the composition realizes, he is safe for now. The restaurant's waiters and habitués appear oblivious to the symbolic danger.

PLATE 32

Eden, 2010
Series: Paradise
Oil on canvas
63 ¾ x 69 ½ (161.9 x 176.5)
Courtesy of the artist and Corbett vs. Dempsey Gallery, Chicago

Barnes tells the Genesis story, from joy in the Garden of Eden to the ultimate fall from grace. Amidst a profusion of lush foliage and exotic fauna, Adam and Eve frolic in the distance, then huddle together in shame in the foreground brush, covering their nakedness after being expelled from the Garden. The loss of immortality is symbolized by the snake about to eat the mouse and by a human skull, a *memento mori*, reminding all of the inevitability of death.

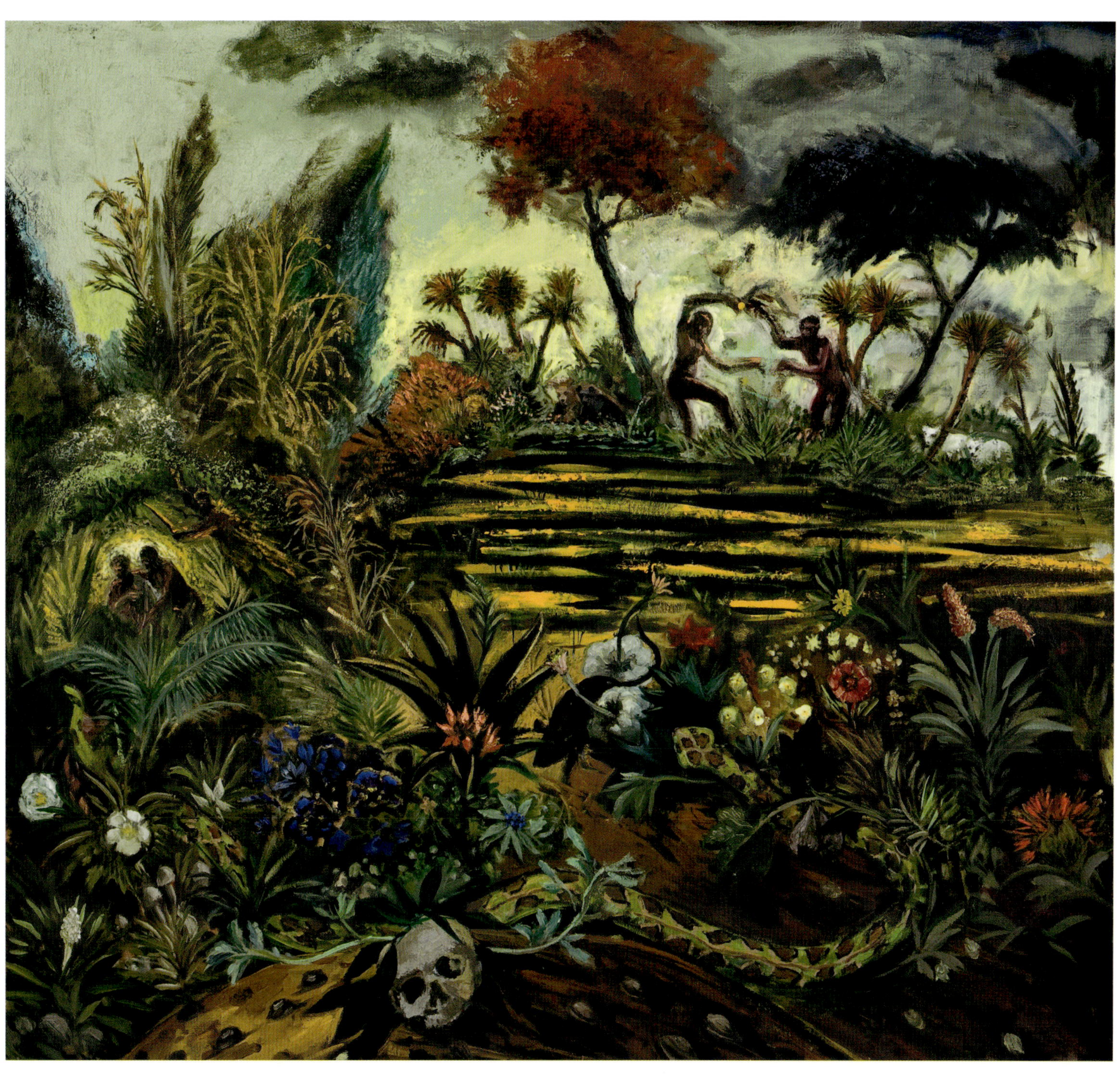

PLATE 33

Mag Mell, 2010
Series: Paradise
Oil on canvas
63 ¾ x 69 ½ (161.9 x 176.5)
Collection of the Indiana University Art Museum, Museum purchase with funds from the Jacqueline O'Brien Art Acquisition Fund and the Elisabeth P. Myers Art Acquisition Endowment Fund, 2010.84

In Celtic mythology, paradise lies on an island to the west of Ireland, or in a kingdom under the sea. In this image a boatload of travelers embarks on their journey to Mag Mell, a place of immortality, beauty, and happiness accessible only to a select few. Sacred fish (related to the legend of Finn McCool and the Salmon of Knowledge, see plate 4) leap in the center of the image, while mistletoe suggests strength and power. Under a coral-colored reef, a beautiful aquatic world can be glimpsed. Rather than the destination, Barnes shows the journey—paradise is represented in the background as a dot of glowing yellow light.

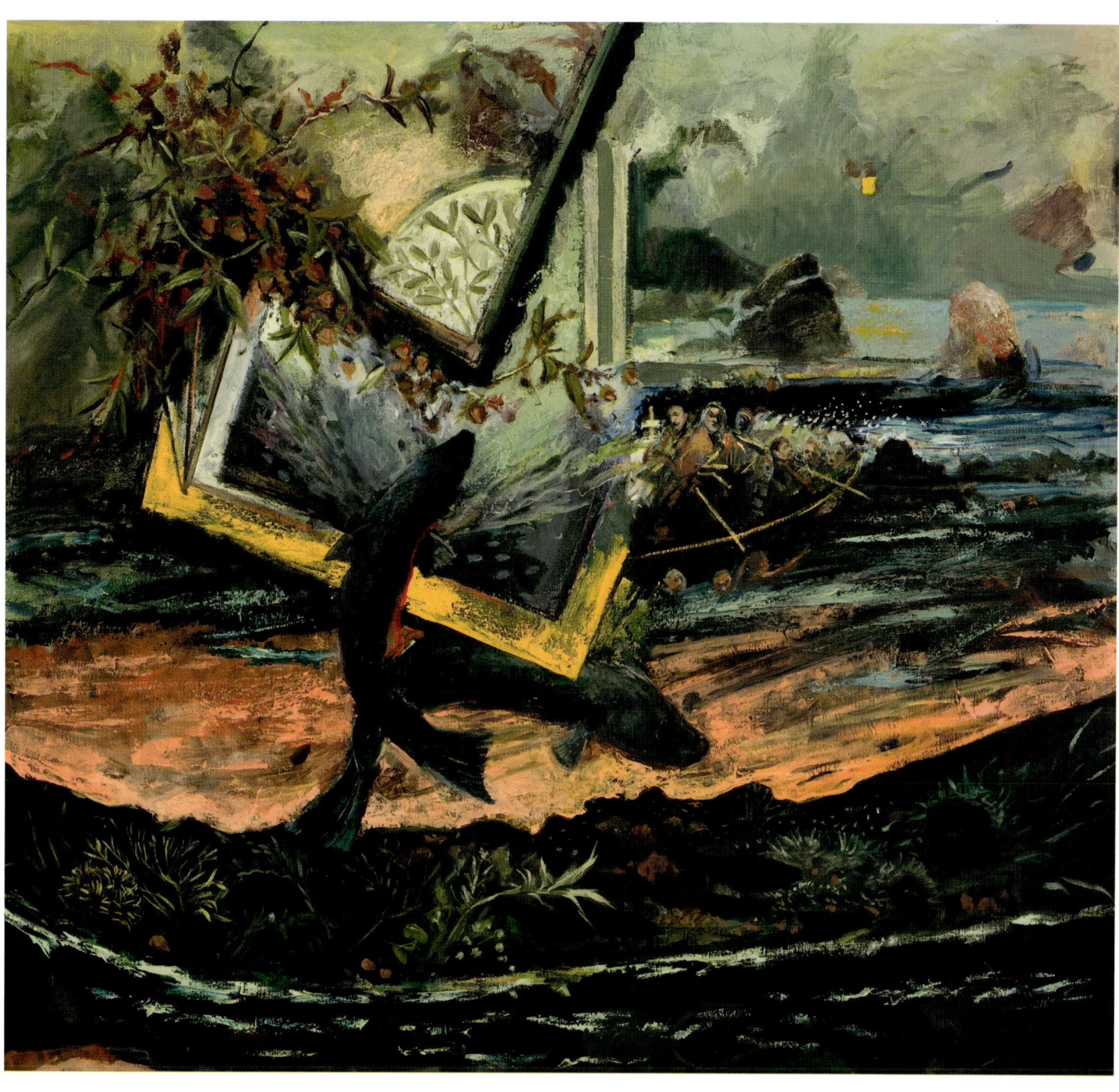

PLATE 34

Arcadia, 2010

Series: Paradise

Oil on canvas

63 ¾ x 69 ½ (161.9 x 176.5)

Courtesy of the artist and Corbett vs. Dempsey Gallery, Chicago

Arcadia suggests a cerebral, ritualized version of paradise drawn from the classical model of reason and order. In the glowing arch behind a laurel wreath and an altar/tomb bearing the inscription *Et in Acadia ego* (Even in Arcadia, I exist) preside the great philosophers of the past. The calm, balanced composition is organized with right angles and harmonious vignettes featuring figures in thoughtful conversation, the legend of the golden apple, and a Doric Greek temple.

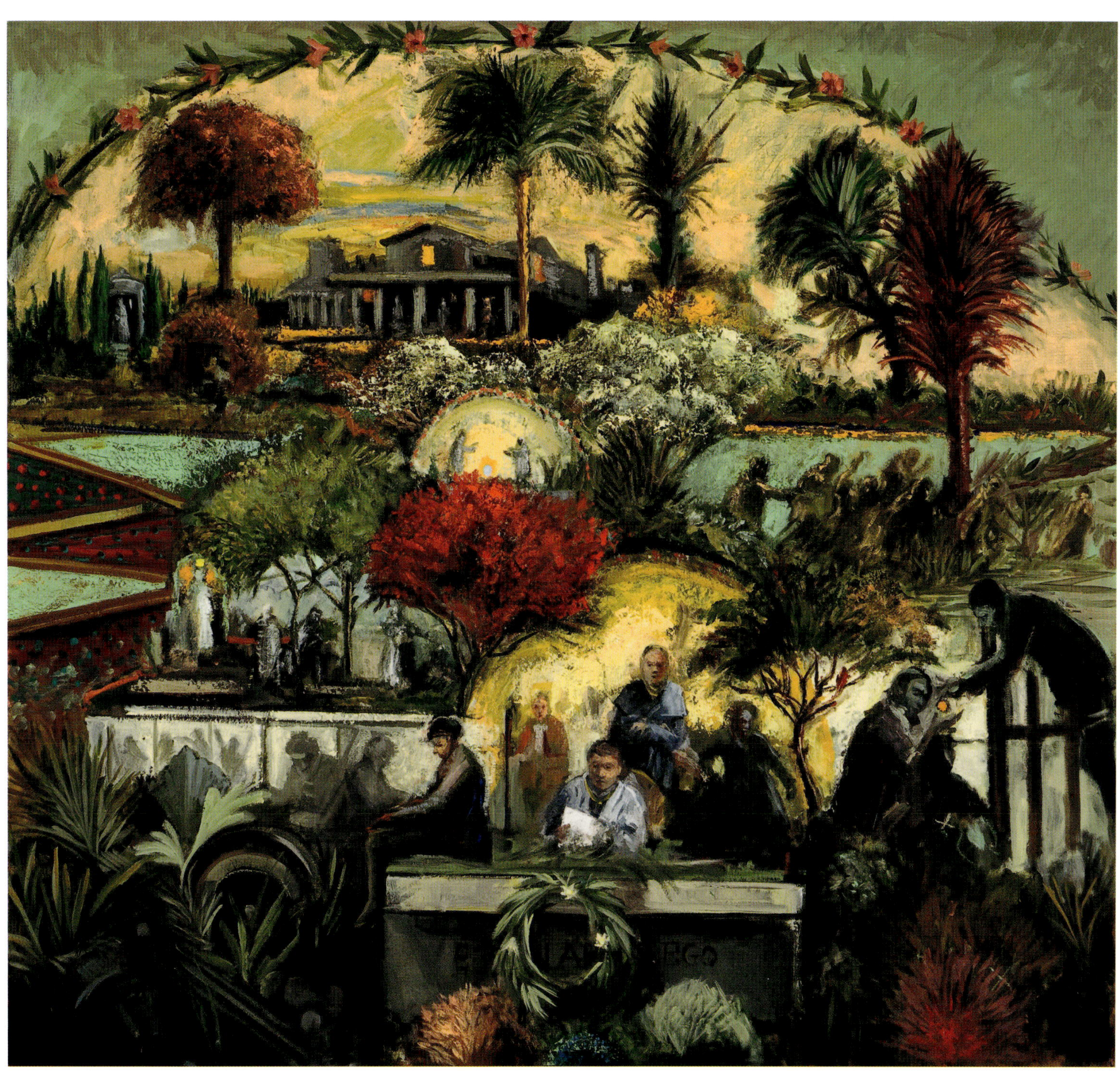

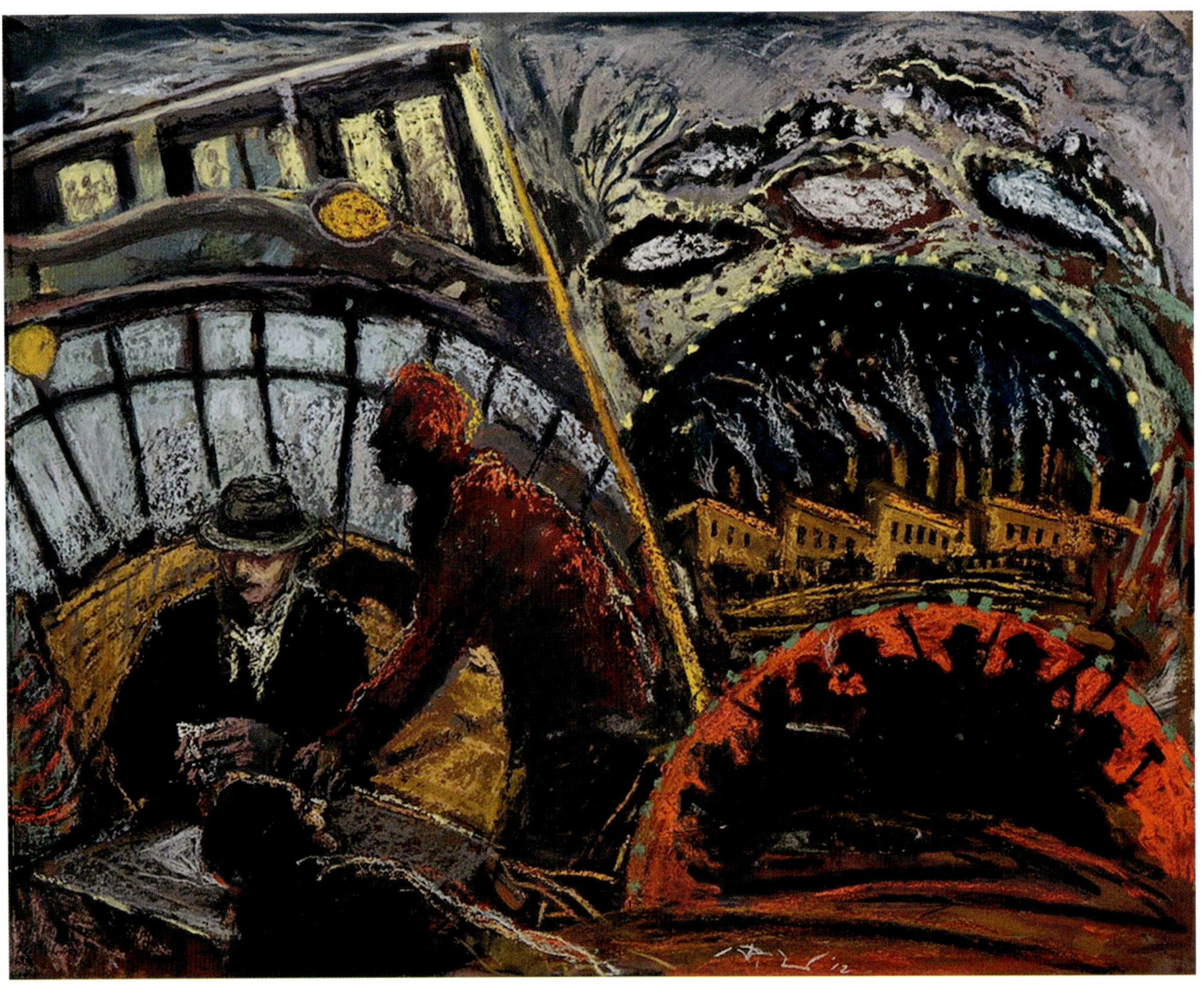

PLATE 35

Wobblies, 2011
Series: The Dil Pickle Club
Pastel and casein on paper
23 x 30 (58.4 x 76.2)
Collection of Rolf Achilles and Maral Hashemi

The Dil Pickle Club, a Bohemian nightspot located in Chicago from 1917 to 1935, was begun by the labor activist John "Jack" Jones. References to its working-class roots are indicated on the right by a line of smoke-belching factories. In the arch below, a silhouetted mass of workers, tools held aloft, represent the Wobblies, members of the radical Industrial Workers of the World (IWW) union, and the Haymarket Riot. On the left, three men plot a future labor agitation.

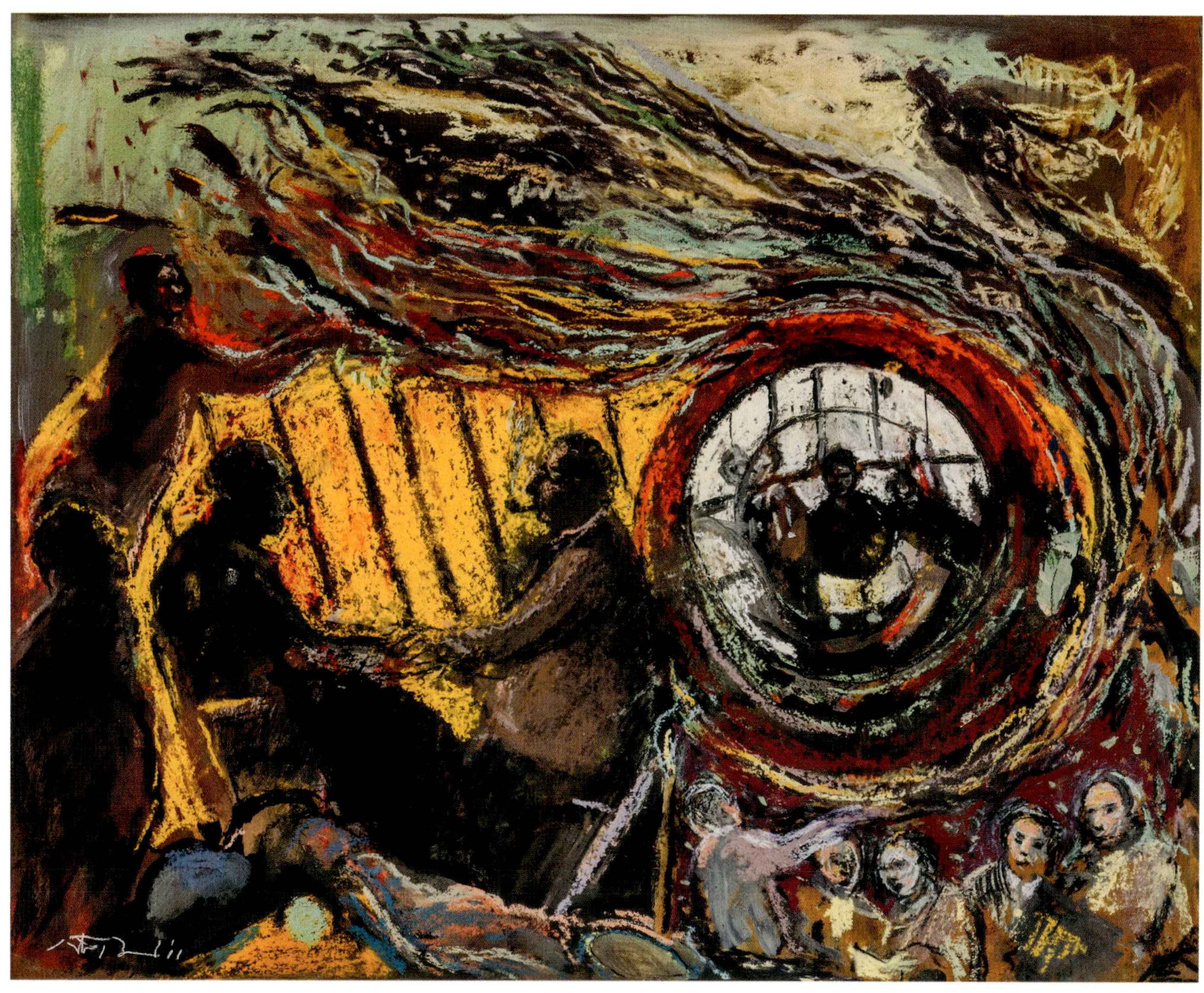

PLATE 36

Poetry Reading at the Dil, 2012
Series: The Dil Pickle Club
Pastel and casein on paper
22 9⁄16 x 30 (57.3 x 76.2)
Collection of the Indiana University Art Museum; Museum purchase with funds from the Estate of Herman B Wells via the Joseph Granville and Anna Bernice Wells Memorial Fund, 2012.41

This scene shows the stimulating atmosphere of the Dil Pickle Club. Although it depicts a poetry reading as seen reflected in the convex mirror surrounded by a fireball of creativity, the image also hints at the club's diverse range of social activities, with a dancing figure in the upper left; a group of people attending a lecture on free sex in the lower right; and a pair of seated men (Maxwell Bodenheim and Carl Sandburg) debating art, science, culture, or politics near the center. Among the club's other noted attendees were Clarence Darrow, Upton Sinclair, Sherwood Anderson, Emma Goldman, and William Carlos Williams.

PLATE 37

Honeymoon on Lake Michigan, 2012
Series: The Dil Pickle Club
Pastel and casein on paper
22 3⁄16 x 29 7⁄8 (56.4 x 75.9)
Collection of the Indiana University Art Museum, Bloomington; Museum purchase with funds from the Estate of Herman B Wells via the Joseph Granville and Anna Bernice Wells Memorial Fund, 2012.42

This image recalls the true story of the doomed honeymoon of John "Jack" Jones, the Dil Pickle Club's founder. He'd built a small boat, and when he married his young girlfriend he decided to take her out on Lake Michigan. Unfortunately, he did not heed the warnings of his comrades on the bridge in the upper-left-hand corner, and the boat sank. While both tried to swim to shore, only Jones made it. This scene depicts the moment just prior to the tragedy with the spirits of those lost at sea coming up from the depths to claim his bride. Jones was blamed for killing her, but ultimately he was exonerated.

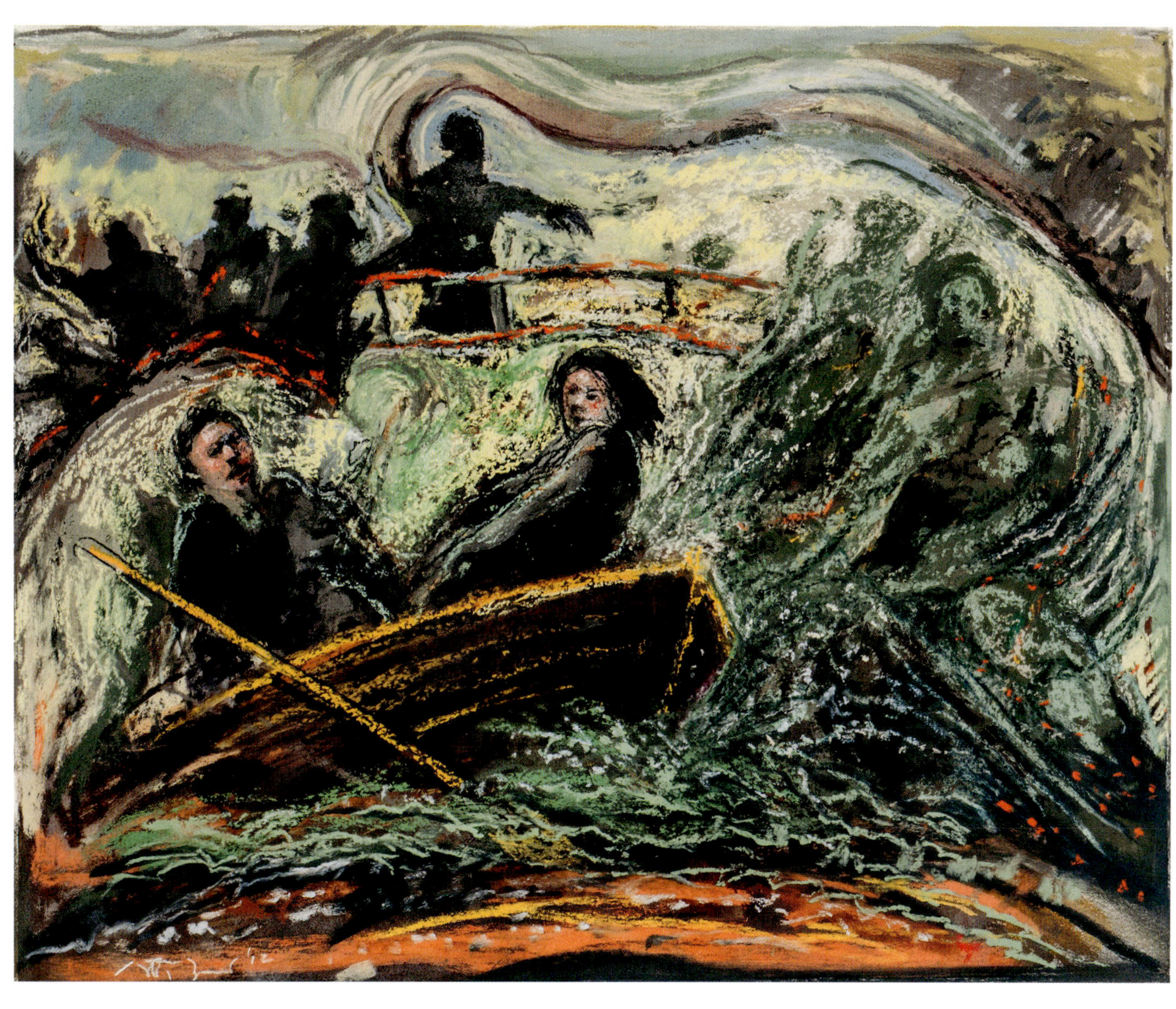

PLATE 38

Tosca/Puccini, 2015
Series: A Night at the Opera
Pastel and casein on paper
23 x 30 (58.4 x 76.2)
Collection of Bill and Kay Carmichael

This colorful drawing shows a progressive re-telling of the final act in Puccini's melodramatic opera *Tosca*. In the lower register the republican artist Mario Cavaradossi stands tied to a stake before a group of stoic monks looking on from under the stage. An allegory of justice with her scales appears in a medallion above them flanked by a judge and a bailiff. In order to save his life, Cavaradossi's lover Floria Tosca has made a pact with the sadistic chief of police to have him shot with blanks by the firing squad in exchange for sex. The white-draped figure of Tosca is shown running through a flaming sky and tossing herself off of the parapet after finding out that she was tricked and that Cavaradossi was actually killed.

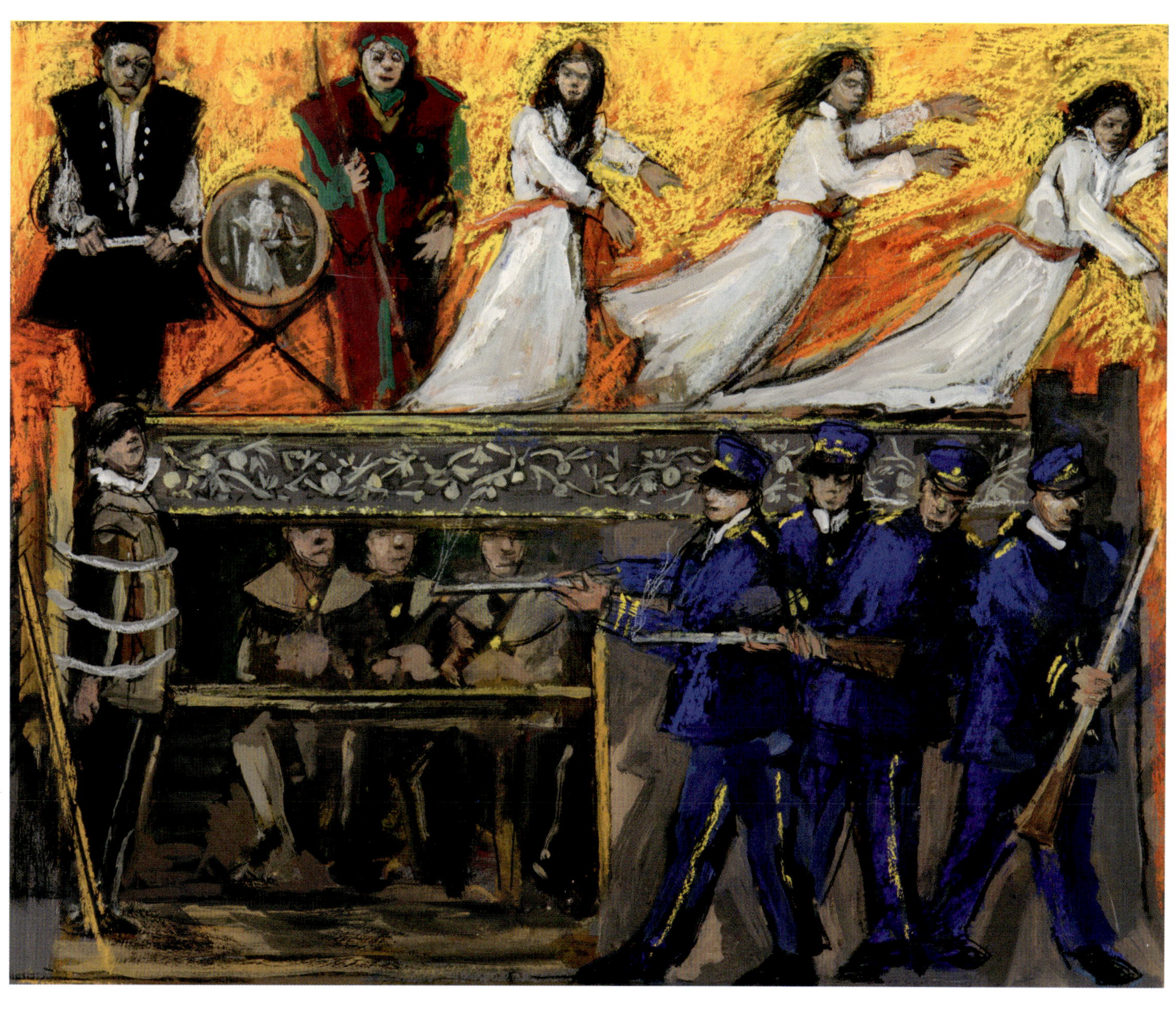

CHRONOLOGY, EXHIBITION HISTORY, AND BIBLIOGRAPHY

1934 Born September 24 in Washington DC to Mahlon and Marjorie Barnes

1952 Graduates from New Trier High School, Winnetka, Illinois, and begins attending the School of the Art Institute of Chicago; meets art dealer Allan Frumkin at one of his first exhibitions and works for Frumkin Gallery during student years

1956 Receives BFA from the School of the Art Institute of Chicago/University of Chicago

1957 Marries fellow art student Lia Sayers; moves to New York City to study; in the late 1950s meets and works as an assistant to the Chilean painter Roberto Matta; through this relationship is involved with the circle of Marcel Duchamp, including Max Ernst, William and Noma Copley, Hans Richter, and the art dealer Julien Levy; becomes involved with the James Joyce Society at Gotham Book Mart

1960 Has first one-man show, at Frumkin Gallery in Chicago; Frumkin becomes his dealer in Chicago and New York

1961 Sails with wife on the QE2 to live and study in London; during his time in England befriends Pop artists including Richard Hamilton, Richard Smith, Peter Blake, and Joe Tilson

1962 First child, a daughter, is born in Kingston upon Thames, England

1963 Moves to Kansas City, Missouri, to teach at Kansas City Art Institute

1964 Accepts teaching position at Indiana University, Bloomington; second child, a son is born

1971 Divorced from Lia Sayers

1972 Marries artist Nancy Morgan; invited by Italian art dealer Mario Roncaglia to come to Italy; lives and works in Umbria, Italy, during a two-year sabbatical from IU; purchases a country house located in Monteacuto, near Umbertide in the Umbrian mountains

1974 Returns to Bloomington; third child, a daughter is born

1979 Fourth child, a daughter is born

1970s Travels with his family as often as possible to Umbria to restore the house and rejoin Italian friends

1985 Spends a year-long IU sabbatical in Umbria

1996 Sonia Zaks becomes his dealer in Chicago

1999 Retires from IU

2001 With wife Nancy, relocates to Searsport, Maine, where they purchase a 180-year-old shipbuilder's house

2015 Establishes the Barnes Artist Residency at the Umbria house

EDUCATION

1952 New Trier High School, Winnetka, Illinois

1956 Bachelor of Fine Arts, School of the Art Institute of Chicago; Bachelor of Fine Arts, University of Chicago; attended Columbia College, New York

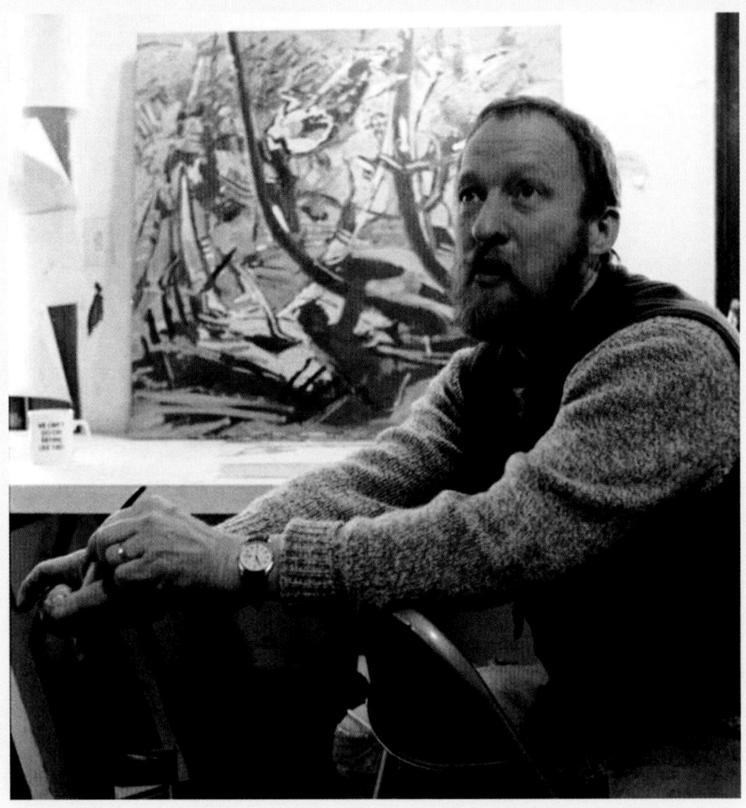

Jerry Mitchell for IU News Bureau, **Portrait of Robert M. Barnes**, January 4, 1983, gelatin silver print, courtesy IU Archives

1957 Hunter College, New York

1963 University of London, Slade School of Art; mentored by Sir William Coldstream and Francis Bacon

TEACHING

1963 Visiting artist position at the Kansas Art Institute, Kansas City, Missouri

1964 Accepts tenure-track position in the Department of Fine Arts, Indiana University, Bloomington

1964-70 IU Assistant Professor of Fine Arts, Painting and Drawing

1970-72 IU Associate Professor of Fine Arts, Painting and Drawing

1972-94 IU Professor of Fine Arts, Painting and Drawing

1994 Named IU Ruth N. Halls Professor of Fine Arts, Endowed Chair

1999 Retires as IU Ruth N. Halls Professor of Fine Art Emeritus

AWARDS

1961 William and Noma Copley Foundation Prize for Painting

1962 Fulbright grant to study English portraiture at the Slade School of Art, University of London

1962 *Art in America* New Talent Award

1963 Art Institute of Chicago, Guri Seaver Award

1963 Fulbright grant renewed

1970 American Academy of Arts and Letters, Childe Hassam Purchase Prize

1982 National Endowment for the Arts Grant

2001 Elected into the American Academy of Design

EXHIBITIONS

One-Person Shows

2015 *Grand Allusions: Robert Barnes—Late Works 1985–2015,* Indiana University Art Museum, Bloomington

2015 *Robert Barnes: A Night at the Opera,* Printworks Gallery, Chicago

2014 *Vicky's Bags,* Works Bookstore and Gallery, Searsport, Maine

2012 *Robert Barnes: Homage to the Dil Pickle Club (New Pastel Drawings),* Printworks Gallery, Chicago

2010 *Robert Barnes: Paradise,* Corbett vs. Dempsey Gallery, Chicago

2009 *Robert Barnes: New Drawings,* Printworks Gallery, Chicago

2006 *Robert Barnes: New Drawings,* Printworks Gallery, Chicago

2004 *Robert Barnes: Jettatura (Amulets, Charms, and Curses),* Sonia Zaks Gallery, Chicago

2002 *Robert Barnes: New Oils and Caseins (The Penobscot),* Sonia Zaks Gallery, Chicago

2000 *Robert Barnes: The Ogham (New Paintings),* Sonia Zaks Gallery, Chicago

2000 *Robert Barnes: Lunch Bags,* IU Hope School of Fine Arts Gallery, Bloomington

1998 *Robert Barnes: New Works,* Sonia Zaks Gallery, Chicago

1997 *Robert Barnes,* College of DuPage, Glen Ellyn, Illinois

1996 *Blood and Perfume: New Paintings,* Sonia Zaks Gallery, Chicago

1992 *Robert Barnes: The Sources of Power,* Struve Gallery, Chicago

1990 *Robert Barnes: Watercolors,* Indiana University Art Museum, Bloomington

1989 *Robert Barnes: Watercolors,* Struve Gallery, Chicago

1986 Natasha Nicholson Gallery, Madison, Wisconsin

1986 Renaissance Society, University of Chicago

1986 *Robert Barnes,* Struve Gallery, Chicago

1985-86 *Robert Barnes 1956–1984: A Survey,* Artists' Choice Museum, New York; Herron Gallery, Indianapolis Center for Contemporary Art; Madison Art Center, Madison, Wisconsin; Hyde Park Art Center and Renaissance Society, Chicago; Art Museum at Florida International University, Miami

1985 Allan Frumkin Gallery, New York

1984 Frumkin/Struve Gallery, Chicago

1983 Allan Frumkin Gallery, New York

1981 Frumkin/Struve Gallery, Chicago

1979 *Robert Barnes: New Paintings and Works on Paper,* Allan Frumkin Gallery, New York

1978 Marianne Friedland Gallery, Toronto

1978 Allan Frumkin Gallery, Chicago

1977 Allan Frumkin Gallery, New York

1975 Allan Frumkin Gallery, New York

1974 *Robert Barnes,* Galleria La Parisina, Torino, Italy

1973 *Robert Barnes,* Galleria Il Fante di Spade, Rome

1971 Allan Frumkin Gallery, Chicago

1970-73 *Robert Barnes: Fifty Watercolors,* Quincy Art Club, Quincy, Illinois; David Strahn Gallery, Jacksonville, Florida; Georgia Museum of Art, Athens; Krannert Art Museum, University of Illinois, Urbana-Champaign; Western Illinois University, Macomb; Illinois State University, Normal; Eastern Kent University, Richmond, Illinois; Springfield Art Association, Springfield, Illinois; Civic Fine Art Association, Sioux Falls; Indiana University Art Museum, Bloomington

1969 Allan Frumkin Gallery, New York

1968 Herron Gallery, Indianapolis Center for Contemporary Art

1967 Galerie du Dragon, Paris

1967 Herron Gallery of Art, Indianapolis; Coe College, Cedar Rapids, Iowa

1966 Reed College, Portland, Oregon

1966 *Barnes, Peintures Récentes,* Galerie du Dragon, Paris

1965 *Barnes–Markman,* Indiana University Art Museum, Bloomington

1965 Rockford College, Rockford, Illinois

1965 Allan Frumkin Gallery, New York

1964 Allan Frumkin Gallery, Chicago

1963 Allan Frumkin Gallery, New York

1960 Allan Frumkin Gallery, Chicago

Group Shows

2016 *Monster Roster: Existentialist Art in Postwar Chicago*, David and Alfred Smart Museum of Art, University of Chicago

2014 *Serial Drawings: Robert Barnes, Barbara Rossi, Robert Lucy*, David and Alfred Smart Museum of Art, University of Chicago

2012 *Face Forward: The Art of the Self-Portrait,* Printworks Gallery, Chicago

2012 *Of, To, and From Ray Yashida,* Pennsylvania Academy of the Fine Arts, Philadelphia

2010 American Academy of Arts and Letters, New York

2006 *Art in Chicago: Resisting Regionalism, Transforming Modernism,* Pennsylvania Academy of the Fine Arts, Philadelphia

2004 *Pastel Society of America 32nd Annual Exhibition,* National Arts Club, New York

2003 *The Exquisite Snake*, Jean Albano Gallery, Chicago

2000 *Fort Wayne Museum of Art Biennial,* Fort Wayne, Indiana

1999 *An Artistic Community: Hope School of Fine Arts Biennial Faculty Show,* Indiana University Art Museum, Bloomington

1998 *Recent Acquisitions: Modern and Contemporary Art,* David and Alfred Smart Museum of Art, University of Chicago

1996 *Don Baum Says Chicago Has Famous Artists,* Hyde Park Art Center, Chicago

1996 *Second Sight: Printmaking in Chicago, 1935–1995,* Block Gallery, Northwestern University, Evanston, Illinois

1996 *A Century of Art: 100th Anniversary of the Henry Radford Hope School of Fine Arts,* Indiana University Art Museum, Bloomington

1995 *Selections from the Toni Gutfreund Collection,* Visual Arts Center, Oakton Community College, Chicago

1994-5 *Chicago Imagism: A 25 Year Survey,* Davenport Museum of Art, Davenport, Iowa

1994 *Still Working, Underknown Artists of Age in America,* Corcoran Gallery of Art, Washington, DC; Chicago Cultural Center; New School for Social Research and Parsons School of Design, New York; Virginia Beach Center for the Arts, Virginia Beach; Fisher Gallery, University of Southern California, Los Angeles; Portland Art Museum, Portland, Oregon

1993 *Celebrating SoFA: Hope School of Fine Arts Biennial Faculty Show*, Indiana University Art Museum, Bloomington

1991 *School of Fine Arts Faculty Exhibition,* Indiana University Art Museum, Bloomington

1989 *School of Fine Arts Faculty Exhibition,* Indiana University Art Museum, Bloomington

1988 *A State of Art: 19th- and 20th-Century Artists at Work in Indiana*, Indiana University Art Museum, Bloomington

1987 *The Landscape Interpreted: Terra Incognita,* Allan Frumkin Gallery, New York

1984-85 *Twentieth-Century American Drawings: The Figure in Context*, Terra Museum of Art, Evanston, Illinois; Arkansas Art Center, Little Rock; Oklahoma Museum of Art, Oklahoma City; Toledo Museum of Art, Toledo, Ohio; Elvehjem Museum of Art, Madison, Wisconsin; National Academy of Design, New York

1984 Allan Frumkin Gallery, New York

1984 *American Art since 1970,* Whitney Museum of American Art, New York

1984 *Chicago Cross Section,* Trisolini Gallery of Ohio University, Athens

1984 *Indiana Influence: The Golden Age of Indiana Landscape Painting—Indiana's Modern Legacy,* Fort Wayne Museum of Art, Indiana

1984 *Rockford College Midwest Invitational,* Rockford College Clark Arts Center Gallery, Rockford, Illinois

1982 *The Human Figure,* Contemporary Arts Center, New Orleans; Four Arts Center, Governors Square, Tallahassee

1982 The Gallery, Bloomington, Indiana

1982 *Selections from the Dennis Adrian Collection,* Museum of Contemporary Art, Chicago

1982 *Drawing Invitational,* Swain School of Design, William W. Crapo Gallery, New Bedford, Massachusetts

1981 *Childe Hassam Purchase Exhibition,* American Academy Institute of Arts and Letters, New York

1981 *Man: Images on Paper,* Weatherspoon Art Gallery, University of North Carolina, Greensboro

1980 *Whitney Halstead Memorial Exhibition,* School of the Art Institute of Chicago

1980 University of New Mexico, Albuquerque

1980 *Realism and Metaphor,* USF Art Galleries, University of Florida, Tampa; Florida International University, Miami; Jacksonville Art Museum, Jacksonville, Florida

1980 *50th Anniversary,* Whitney Museum of American Art, New York

1979 *100 Artists, 100 Years: Alumni of the School of the Art Institute of Chicago,* Art Institute of Chicago

1979 *Narrative Realism: The 14th Harrison Morris Memorial Exhibition,* Art Association of Newport, Newport, Rhode Island

1979 Hansen-Fuller Gallery, San Francisco

1978 *Chicago: The City and Its Artists 1945–1978,* University of Michigan Museum of Art, Ann Arbor

1978 Allan Frumkin Gallery, Chicago

1977 *Contemporary Figurative Painting in the Midwest,* Madison Art Center, Madison, Wisconsin

1977 *Recent Portraiture,* Renaissance Society, University of Chicago

1977 *Watercolor U.S.A.,* Springfield Art Museum, Springfield, Illinois

1977 Allan Frumkin Gallery, New York

1976 *Stanze: oil, pastelli, acquarelli, desegni, incisioni di Bailey, Barnes, Cano, Carroll, Ceccotti, Cremonini, Ferroni, Guccione, McGarrell, Rosofsky,* Galleria Giulia, Rome

1976 *Visions: Paintings and Sculpture, Distinguished Alumni 1945 to the Present,* School of the Art Institute of Chicago

1976 *In Praise of Space: The Landscape in American Art,* Westminster College, New Wilmington, Pennsylvania

1973 *6 Umbrian Painters,* American Consulate, Rome

1973 *Una Tendenza Americana: Ellen Lanyon, Robert Barnes, Seymour Rosofsky, Irving Petlin, James McGarrell,* Galleria Comunale d'Arte Contemporanea, Arezzo, Italy

1972 Kansas City Art Institute, Missouri

1972 *Chicago Imagist Art,* Museum of Contemporary Art, Chicago; New York Cultural Center, New York

1972 Galleria Il Fante di Spade, Rome

1970 *American Painting 1970*, Virginia Museum of Fine Arts, Richmond

1968 *Fantasy and Figure: Chicago Art Since World War II,* American Federation of Arts, New York (traveling exhibition)

1968 *Ravinia Festival Art Exhibit*, Highland Park, Illinois

1968 *Richard J. Daley Exhibition*, Richard Feigen Gallery, Chicago

1967 *Contemporary American Painting and Sculpture,* Krannert Art Museum, University of Illinois, Urbana-Champaign

1967 Allan Frumkin Gallery, Chicago

1967 *Art on Paper Invitational 67,* Weatherspoon Art Gallery, University of North Carolina, Greensboro; University of Wisconsin, Madison

1966 *Il Presente Contesto,* Museo Civico, Bologna, Italy

1966 *161st Annual Exhibition,* Pennsylvania Academy of the Fine Arts, Philadelphia

1966 *Recent Still Life Painting and Sculpture,* Museum of Art, Rhode Island School of Design, Providence

1965 *25: A Tribute to Henry Radford Hope*, Indiana University Art Museum, Bloomington

1965 *Figurative International,* American Federation of the Arts, New York (traveling exhibition)

1965 *Painting and Sculpture Today,* Indianapolis Museum of Art

1965 *50 Artists, 50 States,* Burpee Art Gallery, Rockford, Illinois

1965 Parrish Art Museum, Southampton, New York

1965 Salon de la Jeune Peintres, Paris

1965 Germantown Art Association, Germantown, Pennsylvania

1965 *Art '65*, art show traveled throughout Indiana

1965 *Young America 1965: Thirty American Artists Under Thirty-Five,* Whitney Museum of American Art, New York

1964 *67th Annual American Exhibition,* Art Institute of Chicago

1964 Louisiana State University, Baton Rouge

1964 *Paintings and Constructions of the 1960's Selected from the Richard Brown Baker Collection,* Museum of Art, Rhode Island School of Design, Providence

1963 Allan Frumkin Gallery, New York

1963 *60 Modern Drawings: Recent Acquisitions,* Museum of Modern Art, New York

1963 *Directions: American Painting,* San Francisco Museum of Fine Arts

1963 *23rd Annual Exhibition by the Society for Contemporary American Art,* Art Institute of Chicago
1962 *Huit artistes de Chicago,* Galerie du Dragon, Paris
1962 *Figurative Painting,* Kansas City Art Institute, Missouri
1962 *New Acquisitions,* Whitney Museum of American Art, New York
1962 *Contemporary Paintings Selected from 1960–61 New York Gallery Exhibitions,* Yale University Art Gallery, New Haven, Connecticut
1962 William Rockhill Nelson Gallery of Art, Kansas City, Missouri
1962-63 *Forty Artists under Forty from the Collection of the Whitney Museum of American Art,* Whitney Museum of American Art, New York; Munson-Williams-Proctor Institute, Utica, New York; Rochester Memorial Art Gallery, Rochester, New York; Robertson Memorial Center, Binghamton, New York; Albany Institute of History and Art, Albany, New York; Everson Museum of Art, Syracuse, New York; Andrew Dickson White Museum of Art, Cornell University, Ithaca, New York; Albright-Knox Art Gallery, Buffalo, New York
1961 *Annual Exhition of Contemporary American Painting,* Whitney Museum of American Art, New York
1961 *64th American Exhibition, Paintings, Sculpture,* Art Institute of Chicago
1961 David Herbert Gallery, New York
1961 *Ravinia Festival Art Exhibit*, Highland Park, Illinois
1961 University of Colorado, Boulder
1961 Indiana University Art Museum, Bloomington
1960 *Main Currents of Contemporary American Painting,* University of Iowa, Iowa City
1960 *Annual American Exhibition,* Art Institute of Chicago
1960 *Society for Contemporary American Art,* Art Institute of Chicago
1959 *Ravinia Festival Art Exhibit,* Highland Park, Illinois
1958 *Society for Contemporary American Art,* Art Institute of Chicago
1957 *Annual American Exhibition,* Art Institute of Chicago
1957 6th Annual Boston Arts Festival
1956 University of Chicago
1956 Rockford College, Illinois
1955 *Prints from the Graphic Workshop,* Art Institute of Chicago
1955 *Cliff Dwellers Print Exhibition,* Cliff Dwellers Club, Chicago
1954 *Exhibition Momentum,* Institute of Design, Chicago
1953 *Exhibition Momentum, Mid-Continental,* Werner's Bookstore, Chicago
1952 *Exhibition Momentum, Mid-Continental,* Werner's Bookstore, Chicago

BIBLIOGRAPHY

Books and Articles

"Acquisitions, July 1, 2007–June 30, 2008." *Yale University Art Gallery Bulletin*, 2008, 200.

Adrian, Dennis. *Chicago Imagism: A 25 Year Survey*. Davenport, Iowa: Davenport Museum of Art, 1994.

———. *Robert Barnes 1956–1984: A Survey*. Madison, Wisconsin: Madison Art Center, 1984.

———. *Robert Barnes: Fifty Watercolors*. Quincy, Illinois: Quincy Art Club, 1970.

———. *Selections from the Dennis Adrian Collection*. Chicago: Museum of Contemporary Art, 1982.

———. *Sight Out of Mind: Essays and Criticism on Art*. Ann Arbor: UMI Research Press, 1985.

———. *Visions: Painting and Sculpture: Distinguished Alumni 1945 to the Present.* Chicago: School of the -Art Institute of Chicago, 1976.

Annual Exhibition of Contemporary American Painting. New York: Whitney Museum of American Art, 1961.

Art on Paper Invitational 67. Greensboro, North Carolina: Weatherspoon Art Gallery, 1967.

Baker, Richard Brown. *Paintings and Constructions of the 1960's Selected from the Richard Brown Baker Collection.* Providence, Rhode Island: Museum of Art, Rhode Island School of Design, 1964.

"Birch Bayh Honors Artists at Washington Reception." *Indiana Daily Student,* September 15, 1965.

Bowie, Theodore. *25: A Tribute to Henry Radford Hope*. Bloomington, Indiana: School of Fine Arts, 1965.

Carlson, Valerie. "Fine Arts Professor Paints His Way to Fame and Fortune." *Indiana Daily Student,* April 11, 1983.

Carluccio, Luigi. *Robert Barnes.* Rome: Galleria Il Fante di Spade, 1971

———. *Robert Barnes.* Torino, Italy: Galleria La Parisina, 1974.

———. *Una Tendenza Americana: Ellen Lanyon, Robert Barnes, Seymour Rosofsky, Irving Petlin, James McGarrell.* Arezzo, Italy: Galleria Comunale d'Arte Contemporanea, 1973.

Chicago Imagist Art. Chicago: Museum of Contemporary Art, 1972.

Clarac-Sérou, Max. *Robert Barnes: Peintures Récentes.* Paris: Galerie du Dragon, 1966.

Cloe, Vanessa. "Whatever Happened to...?: The College Catches Up with Some Favorite Faculty Members from Years Past." *The College* 29, no. 1 (summer 2005): 5.

Contemporary Figurative Painting in the Midwest: An Invitational Exhibition at the Madison Art Center. Madison, Wisconsin: Madison Art Center, 1977.

Cozzolino, Robert. *Art in Chicago: Resisting Regionalism, Transforming Modernism*. Philadelphia: Pennsylvania Academy of the Fine Arts, 2007.

Cummings, Paul. *Twentieth-Century American Drawings: The Figure in Context*. Washington, DC: International Exhibitions Foundation, 1984.

Exhibition Momentum. Chicago Momentum Group, 1954.

Exhibition Momentum Mid-Continental. Chicago Momentum Group, 1953.

Exhibition Momentum Mid-Continental. Chicago Momentum Group, 1952.

Frank, Peter. *Indiana Influence: The Golden Age of Indiana Landscape Painting, Indiana's Modern Legacy: An Inaugural Exhibition of the Fort Wayne Museum of Art.* (Curated by William H. Gerdts). Fort Wayne, Indiana: Fort Wayne Museum of Art, 1984.

Girst, Thomas. "'A very normal guy': An Interview with Robert Barnes on Marcel Duchamp and État Donnés," *The Marcel Duchamp Studies Online Journal* 2, no. 4 (January 2002) http://www.toutfait.com.

Godfrey, Robert. *In Praise of Space: The Landscape in American Art.* New Wilmington, Pennsylvania: Westminster College, 1976.

Goodrich, Lloyd. *Young America 1965: Thirty American Artists Under Thirty-Five.* New York: Whitney Museum of American Art, 1965.

Goodrich, Lloyd. and Edward Bryant. *Forty Artists Under Forty, from the Collection of the Whitney Museum of American Art.* New York: Praeger, 1962.

Halls, Doris. "An Interview with Robert Barnes." *Steppin Out* (February 1986): 20–21.

Hawkins, Margaret. "In a Mirror, Squintingly," in *Face Forward: The Art of the Self-Portrait*. Chicago: Printworks Gallery, 2012.

"IU Prof Receives NEA Artist Grant." *IU Newspaper* (June 1983).

Kapslis, Terry. "Candy and Concubines for Robert Barnes," in *Robert Barnes: Paradise.* Chicago: Corbett vs. Dempsey, 2010.

Kozloff, Max. "Inwardness: Chicago Art Since 1945." *Artforum* 11, no. 2 (October 1972): 51–55.

Kroutel, Ron. *Chicago Cross Section.* Athens, Ohio: Trisolini Gallery of Ohio University, 1984.

Lee, Hon-ching, and Sonja Rae. *Whitney Halstead Memorial Exhibition.* Chicago: School of the Art Institute of Chicago, 1980.

Main Currents of Contemporary American Painting. Iowa City: University of Iowa, 1960.

Marshall, Richard. *American Art since 1970.* New York: Whitney Museum of American Art, 1984.

Martin, Jean. "A Conversation with Robert Barnes." *Allan Frumkin Gallery Newsletter* 20 (Fall 1985): 1, 4–6.

______. "Robert Barnes: Painting and Reading, Reading and Painting." *Allan Frumkin Gallery Newsletter* (Spring 1977): 1–2.

McCrillis, Michele M. "Matta in Chicago: A Reexamination of the Career of Roberto Matta Echaurren in the 1950's." Master's thesis, School of the Art Institute of Chicago, 1992.

McCullough, L. E. "Robert Barnes: Work in Progress." *Arts Indiana* 12, no. 9 (December 1990): 28–32.

Miller, Margaret. *Realism and Metaphor*. Tampa, Florida: SVC Fine Arts Gallery, 1980.

Monett, Alexandra. *The Human Figure.* New Orleans: Contemporary Arts Center, 1982.

1980—The 50th Anniversary of the Whitney Museum of American Art. New York: Whitney Museum of American Art, 1980.

100 Artists, 100 Years: Alumni of the School of the Art Institute of Chicago. Chicago: Art Institute of Chicago, 1979.

161st Annual Exhibition. Philadelphia: Pennsylvania Academy of Fine Arts, 1966.

Parks, John A. "Rough, Dirty, and Dangerous Pastels." *American Artist* 69, no. 751 (February 2005): 46–51.

Quesada, Mario. *Stanze: oil, pastelli, acquarelli, desegni, incisioni di Bailey, Barnes, Cano, Carroll, Ceccotti, Cremonini, Ferroni, Guccione, McGarrell, Rosofsky*. Rome: Galleria Giulia, 1976.

Rockford College Midwest Invitational. Rockford, Illinois: Rockford College Clark Arts Center Gallery, 1984.

Rooks, Michael Allen. "Allusion and Metaphor in Robert Barnes' *Arthur Cravan Still Lives*." Master's thesis, School of the Art Institute of Chicago, 1995.

———. *Robert Barnes*. Glen Ellyn, Illinois: Gahlberg Gallery, College of DuPage, 1997.

———. "Seeking the City of Truth: Robert Barnes's Illustrations for the First Ten *Cantos* of Ezra Pound." *The Smart Museum of Art Bulletin* 8 (1996–97): 8–19.

Schulze, Franz. *Fantastic Images: Chicago Art Since 1945*. Chicago: Follett Publishing Company,1972.

———. *Fantasy and Figure: Chicago Art Since World War II*. New York: American Federation of Arts, 1969.

———. *Huit artistes de Chicago: Barnes–Campoli–Cohen–June Leaf–Golub–Petlin–Rosofsky–Westermann*, Paris: Galerie du Dragon, 1962.

———. "Identities of Postwar Chicago Art: The Image and the Dream." *Chicago Daily News*, 1967.

______. "Reflections on the 50s," *Chicago Daily News*, October 2–3, 1971.

———. "Where Is American Art Going?" *Chicago Daily News*, February 3, 1971.

———. "Where Is American Art Going?" (Conversation with Studs Terkel). *WFMT Perspective* (July 1962): 18–29.

Selz, Peter Howard. *American Painting 1970*. Richmond: Virginia Museum of Fine Arts, 1970.

Shedletsky, Stuart, Larry Fink, Ann Eden Gibson, and Corcoran Gallery of Art. *Still Working: Underknown Artists of Age in America*. Providence, Rhode Island: Parsons School of Design, New York, in association with University of Washington Press, Seattle and London, 1994.

64th American Exhibition: Paintings, Sculpture. Chicago: Art Institute of Chicago, 1961.

Speyer, A. James. *67th Annual American Exhibition: Directions in Contemporary Painting and Sculpture.* Chicago: Art Institute of Chicago, 1964.

Stoddard, Leah. "Blood, Paint and Perfume." *Arts Indiana* 17, no. 2 (March 17, 1995): 24–25.

Tannenbaum, Barbara. *Chicago: The City and Its Artists 1945–1978*. Edited by Charles A Lewis and Cynthia Yao. Ann Arbor: University of Michigan Museum of Art, 1978.

Union League Club of Chicago Art Collection. Chicago: Union League Club of Chicago, 2003.

Vincent, Edie, and Bob McConnell. "Bayh's Two 'Art Mobiles' to Visit Bloomington." *Indiana Daily Student*, October 2, 1965.

Watercolor U.S.A. Springfield, Illinois: Springfield Art Museum, 1977.

Yood, James. *Second Sight: Printmaking in Chicago,1935–1995*. Evanston, Illinois: Northwestern, 1996.

———. *2000 Biennial*. Fort Wayne, Indiana: Fort Wayne Museum of Art, 2000.

Zirker, Joan. "Painting in a New Place: Bonnie Sklarski and Robert Barnes." *Arts and Sciences* 13, no. 1 (Fall 1989): 6–9.

———. "College Announces Ruth Halls Professorships." *The College* 18, no. 1 (Fall 1994): 6–7.

Reviews

Adrian, Dennis. "Homage to Barnes, American Master." *Chicago Daily News*, January 7–8, 1978.

Ahlander, Leslie Judd. "Barnes Exhibit Fills FIU Gallery with Tension." *Miami News*, September 26, 1986.

Allen, Jane, and Derek Guthrie. "Two New Showings Help Make Some Important Points." *Chicago Tribune*, October 3, 1971.

"Art Show Presents State Talent." *Indiana Daily Student*, October 5, 1965.

Artner, Alan G. "A History that Defeats Itself." *Chicago Tribune*, November 24, 1996.

———. "Barnes Powers Paintings by Deliberation." *Chicago Tribune*, May 8, 1982.

———. "Barnes' Elaborate Pastels Nourish the Eye While Telling Stories." *Chicago Tribune*, April 3, 1998.

———. "Exhibition Circuit Offers Three Worthwhile Stops." *Chicago Tribune*, January 15, 1978.

———. "Fragile Beauty on Display in Avery Collection." *Chicago Tribune*, May 8, 1981.

______. "Re-Introducing Robert Barnes." *Chicago Tribune*, March 29, 2002.

———. "Two-Part Show Irresistibly Robert Barnes." *Chicago Tribune*, August 15, 1986.

"Barnes–Markman Exhibit to Be First Fall Art Show." *Indiana Daily Student*, September 21, 1965.

Barry, Edward. "50 States Show Scores a First." *Chicago Tribune*, October 10, 1965.

Benbow, Charles. "USF Realism Exhibit Is Rated Outstanding." *St. Petersburg Times*, April 27, 1980.

Bracalente, Anita. "Blending of the Artist and His Art." *Sunday Herald-Times,* February 23, 1985.

Burrell, Sherri. "Faculty Artists Tout N.Y. Galleries." *Indiana Daily Student*, September 16, 1977.

Bushyeager, Peter. "Robert Barnes." *New Art Examiner* 13, no. 5 (January 1986): 61–62.

Canaday, John. "Art." *New York Times*, April 20, 1968.

Ciezadlo, Janina. "Review: Robert Barnes/Corbett vs. Dempsey" (May 24, 2010) http://art.newcit.com

Day, Holliday T. "Robert Barnes at Allan Frumkin." *Art in America* 66, no. 5 (September–October, 1978): 131.

Finkelstein, Lydia B. "Barnes' Watercolors [Are] Artist's 'Visual Diary'." *Sunday Herald-Times*, April 29, 1990.

Friedlander, Alberta. "Design, Color, Bold in Barnes Work," *Chicago Daily News*, September 16, 1961.

______. "Chicago's Young Rebel Artists." *Chicago Daily News*, June 17, 1961.

———. "Many Greats, Few Mediocrities: Ravinia Show Is Best." *Chicago Daily News*, July 6, 1959.

———. "Some Memorable Exhibitions." *Chicago Daily News*, December 30, 1961.

Frumkin, Allan. "2 Shows Spotlight Renaissance in Art." *Chicago Daily News*, September 21, 1959.

———. "Barnes Works in Fine Show." *Chicago Daily News*, December 31, 1960.

———. "Fine Prints on Display." *Chicago Daily News*, August 6, 1961.

Gerard, Paul. "It's Not About Art." *Isthmus*, April 18, 1986.

Gerber, Lisa. "Artist's Medium Is Extremes." *Indiana Daily Student*, February 5, 1978.

Giuffre, Guido. "American raffinata." *Sette Giorni*, June 24, 1973.

Glueck, Grace. "Art." *New York Times,* February 25, 1983.

Hayden, Harold. "Explosive Quality in Barnes' Art." *Chicago Sun-Times*, May 22, 1981.

Hoffman, Nan. "Ambiguity Part of Attraction in Robert Barnes' Work." *Indianapolis Star*, February 9, 1986.

Holg, Garrett. "Robert Barnes." *Art News* 91, no. 8 (October 1992): 142.

Holland, Frank. "Barnes Has Exciting Show Here." *Chicago Sun-Times*, December 18, 1960.

———. "Club Shows Easterners' Fine Works." *Chicago Sun-Times*, February 7, 1954.

———. "Momentum Exhibit Falls Below Par." *Chicago Sun-Times*, May 17, 1953.

"Home Are the Artists: Ravinia Shows Us Eight Natives Who Make Good." *Chicago Daily News*, June, 1968

Huebner, Jeff. "Fresh From the Old School: A Member of the Monster Roster Blows Back Into Town." *Chicago Reader* 27, no. 28 (April17, 1998): 8, 10, 12.

"I.U. Dedicates Its Fine Arts to Statewide Cultural Festival." *Indiana Daily Student*, September, 23, 1965.

Knudsen, Stephen. "Random Gallery Spotlight: Corbett vs. Dempsey." *Chicago Art Magazine*, March 13, 2012.

Kohen, Helen L. "Imagination Colors Barnes Show at FIU." *Miami Herald Weekend*, September 19, 1986.

Kozloff, Max. "Barnes." *Art International* 7, no. 10 (Christmas/New Year, 1963–64): 35.

Loudenback, Brad. "Robert Barnes." *New Art Examiner* 13, no. 8 (April 1986): 64.

Martin, Robert. "Current Exhibit at USF Demonstrates that Realism Is the Ultimate in Abstraction." *Tampa Times*, April 29, 1980.

Mascherpa, Giorgio. "Cinque pittori USA e il barocco." *Avvenire*, June 9, 1973.

Micacchi, Dario. "Americani del dissenso." *L'Unita*, June 1, 1973.

Moellering, Caroline. "Professor's Works Focus on Real Life Experiences." *Indiana Daily Student*, April 25, 1990.

Nuzum, Thomas. "Paris Takes a Look at Chicago Art." *Chicago Tribune*, March 25, 1962.

O'Brien, Glenn. "Robert Barnes: Artists' Choice Museum." *Artforum* 24, no. 7 (March 1986): 118.

O'Doherty, Brian. "Art." *New York Times*, November 2, 1963.

Paloscia, Tommaso. "Una Tendenza Americana." *Las Nazione*, June 12, 1973.

Pieszak, Devonna. "Robert Barnes." *New Art Examiner* 7, no. 2 (February 1978): 1–9.

Preston, Stuart. "Art: The Advance Guard." *New York Times*, January 16, 1960.

______. "Art: A Mammoth Week of Exhibitions." *New York Times*, April 10, 1965.

———. "A Good Catch of Drawings." *New York Times*, September 5, 1965.

———. "The Sensation Seekers." *New York Times*, June 27, 1962.

Purdie, James. "A Prelude of High-Stepping Horses: Robert Barnes." *Toronto Globe and Mail*, April 22, 1978.

"Review of Figurative Painting." *Fine Arts Calendar* (October 1962): 22.

Rhea, Tom. "Blood and Perfume: Recent Painting by Robert Barnes." *Arts Indiana* 18, no. 9 (November 1996): 16.

"Robert Barnes." *Art News* 85, no. 2 (February 1986): 125–26.

"Robert Barnes' Lunch Bags at Works in Searsport," *Free Press*, April 2, 2014.

Rodrig uez, Joanne Milani. "The Reality of the Unconscious." *Tampa Tribune-Times*, April 27, 1980.

Rooks, Michael. "Robert Barnes: New Work." *Dialogue* (July/August 1998): 11–12.

Schulze, Franz. "An Old Master and a New Journalist." *Chicago Daily News*, November 23, 1968.

———. "Good Show, Splendid Concept." *Chicago Daily News*, February 28, 1964.

———. "Grosz, Golub, Barnes." *Art News* 60, no. 1 (March 1961): 49, 55.

———. "Spring Brings Bright Look to Art." *Chicago Daily News*, March 31, 1962.

———. "The Drawings Look Drawn." *Chicago Daily News*, June 1974.
———. "Three Painters in Three Styles Go on Exhibit." *Chicago Daily News*, December 19, 1966.
"Show Ready." *Indiana Daily Student*, September 22, 1965.
Taylor, Sue. "Barnes Works His Magic Using Obscure Themes." *Chicago Sun-Times*, August 21, 1986.
———. "Robert Barnes." *Art in America* 75, no. 2 (February 1987): 156–57.
Thomas, Linda. "Strolling through Hoosier exhibit." *Sunday Herald-Times, August 28, 1988*
"Two Barnes Shows." *Chicago* (July 1986): 22.
Vine, Richard. "Robert Barnes at Sonia Zaks." *Art in America* 86, no. 7 (July 1998): 101–102.
Willis, Thomas. "At Ravinia, Art by Native Sons." *Chicago Tribune*, June 30, 1968.

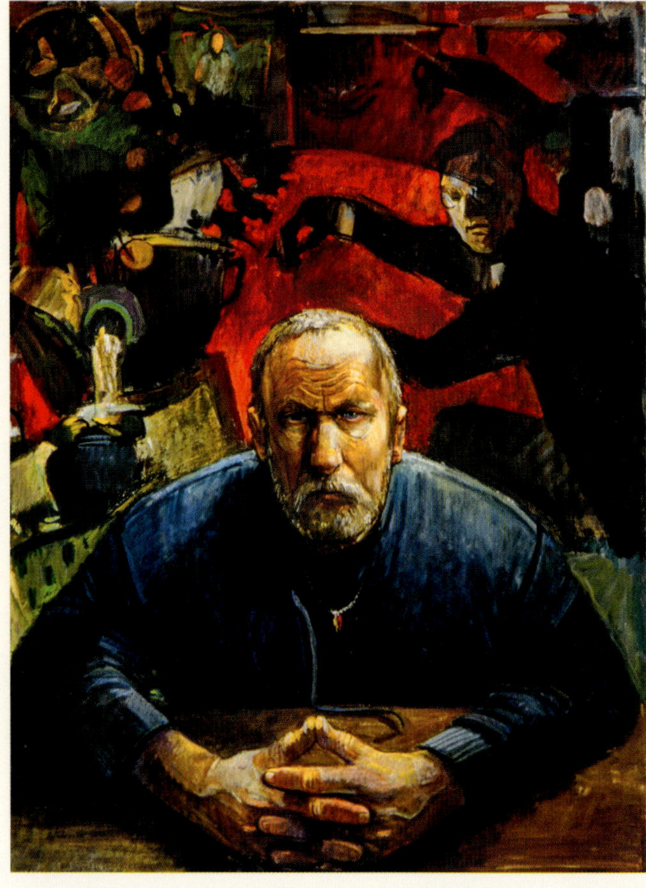

Nancy Morgan Barnes (American, born 1948).
Portrait of Bob [in front of his painting *Molinard-Grasse* (plate 8)], 2000. Oil on panel. Indiana University Art Museum, 2001.1

PUBLIC AND CORPORATE COLLECTIONS

Albrecht-Kemper Museum of Art, St. Joseph, Missouri
Art Institute of Chicago
Block Museum of Art, Northwestern University, Evanston, Illinois
Chazen Museum of Art, University of Wisconsin-Madison
David and Alfred Smart Museum of Art, University of Chicago
DePauw University, Greencastle, Indiana
Indiana State Museum, Indianapolis
Indiana University Art Museum, Bloomington
Indianapolis Museum of Art
Kishwaukee College, Malta, Illinois
MB Financial Bank, N.A., Rosemont, Illinois
Madison Museum of Contemporary Art, Madison, Wisconsin
Museum of Contemporary Art, Chicago
Museum of Modern Art, New York
Springfield Art Museum, Springfield, Missouri
Union League Club of Chicago
Weatherspoon Art Gallery, University of North Carolina at Greensboro
Whitney Museum of American Art, New York
Yale University Art Gallery, New Haven, Connecticut